Navigating Negativity: Strategies for Positive Encounters

Transforming Toxic Interactions into Opportunities for Growth

Sarah Mitchell

Table of Contents

INTRODUCTION

It is a skill and a requirement in a society where negativity can easily find its way into our lives to turn harmful interactions into chances for personal development. It is intended to lead you through the complex process of comprehending and handling negativity. "Navigating Negativity: Strategies for Positive Encounters: Transforming Toxic Interactions into Opportunities for Growth." This book offers helpful tactics to assist you in transforming difficult circumstances into opportunities for relationship and personal growth.

Our emotional health, interpersonal connections, and general quality of life can all be significantly impacted by negativity, whether outside sources or internal conflicts. This book explores the causes of unfavorable interactions and provides insights into the social and psychological elements that support them. Self-awareness and emotional intelligence will help you deal with these difficult situations more skillfully.

This book will teach you practical communication skills, conflict-resolution strategies, and resilience-building techniques. Each chapter is designed to equip you with the skills you need to recognize, confront, and change harmful behaviors in yourself and others, making you feel prepared to navigate negativity constructively.

'Navigating Negativity' is about surviving adversity and thriving in the face of it. By the end of this journey, you will be more than equipped to deal with negativity constructively, leading to a happier and more satisfying existence for you and those around you. This book is a beacon of hope, showing you the transformative potential of every negative encounter.

CHAPTER I

Understanding Negativity

The Origins of Negativity

A ubiquitous feature of human existence, negativity has strong cultural and historical roots that influence how people view and relate to one another in individuals and societies. It is necessary to examine the historical development and artistic expressions of negativity to uncover the common elements that give rise to negative interactions. This section thoroughly explains the causes of negativity and how it affects interpersonal interactions and behavior.

Negativity has its historical roots in prehistoric societies where conflict, distrust, and terror were frequently essential to existence. Predators, other human groups, and the environment all challenged humanity during the prehistoric era. Adverse feelings like dread and rage were critical for warning people about danger and inspiring them to take preventative measures. The species' ability to survive depended on these survival strategies. These automatic reactions grew deeply embedded in the human brain throughout time, playing a role in the formation of negative attitudes and behaviors.

The pervasiveness of negativity in human civilizations is also seen in ancient literature and religious traditions. For example, original sin emphasizes human frailty and moral problems in the Judeo-Christian tradition. This story emphasizes that negativity is a natural aspect of being human and something people should always work to overcome. Similarly, ancient Greek philosophers like Plato and Aristotle examined jealousy, rage, and other negative characteristics of human nature as barriers to leading a moral life. These philosophical discussions paved the way for understanding negativity as a basic aspect of the human condition.

Culturally, negativity takes many forms in diverse countries, each formed by its own social norms, beliefs, and traditions. Negativity can take many forms. It can be overt in certain cultures, where it takes the form of verbal abuse and confrontation, or it can be more covert and take the form of silent resentment or passive-aggressive conduct. For instance, individualism and competition are highly regarded in many Western societies, frequently resulting in hostile relationships motivated by jealousy, rivalry, and the need for personal achievement. While collectivist societies, like those found in East Asia, strongly emphasize harmony and community cohesion, social pressure, guilt, and humiliation can still be present when people don't live up to society's standards.

Contemporary cultural forces further complicate the terrain of negativity. The proliferation of social media and digital communication has magnified and increased the visibility and prevalence of unpleasant encounters. Online venues frequently offer anonymity, lowering accountability and improving people's freedom to voice negativity. Due to this tendency, there is a prevalent culture of negativity in virtual places, which has given rise to cyberbullying, trolling, and other types of digital harassment. Furthermore, persistent exposure to unfavorable news and information via media may heighten dread, anxiety, and mistrust, exacerbating unfavorable encounters in day-to-day contact.

It is necessary to look at society and individual elements to comprehend the common causes of unfavorable relationships. Individual differences in psychological characteristics and experiences greatly impact how people react to adverse stimuli. Unpleasant behaviors and attitudes can be predisposed by personality traits like neuroticism, which is marked by emotional instability and a propensity to experience unpleasant emotions. Trauma, abuse, and neglect during childhood can all leave long-lasting effects that influence how people view and respond to negative things. These formative encounters can contribute to a cycle of unfavorable interactions that lasts into adulthood by fostering feelings of distrust, insecurity, and hate.

Cognitive processes greatly aid the persistence of negativity. People who are susceptible to cognitive biases, such the negativity bias, tend to focus more on and weigh negative information more heavily than positive information. Due to this prejudice, people may see situations that are unclear or benign behaviors as aggressive or menacing. In a similar vein, attributional styles—that is, how people interpret the reasons behind events—can impact negativity. Pessimistic attributional styles reinforce feelings of powerlessness and resentment by attributing unpleasant events to stable, external, and internal sources.

Negative encounters are more common because of social dynamics. Social hierarchies, rivalry for resources, and power disparities can all foster an atmosphere conducive to negative. Hierarchical systems and competitive cultures may encourage employee backstabbing, jealousy, and competition in the workplace. Concerns about one's standing and reputation in social groups can give rise to bullying, exclusion, and gossip. In addition, societal problems like injustice, discrimination, and inequality can cause a generalized negative sentiment because they make marginalized groups feel angry, frustrated, and disenchanted with the way things are.

Stereotypes and cultural narratives intensify negativity even further. Prejudice and discrimination can result from stereotypes, which are oversimplified and generalized ideas about specific populations. Cultural narratives and media portrayals frequently reinforce these unfavorable attitudes, feeding prejudices and fostering unfavorable interactions. Racial and ethnic prejudices, for instance, can lead to systematic discrimination, which impacts people's opportunities, experiences, and relationships in a variety of social settings.

Negativity is mostly shaped by the family, which is also a major socialization factor. Family dynamics impact how people learn to manage negative emotions and situations. These dynamics include parenting styles, communication patterns, and conflict resolution techniques. Children raised by authoritarian parents—who enforce rigid rules and severe penalties—may develop anxiety and resentment as well as undesirable behavioral tendencies. On the other hand, aggressive behavior and a lack of self-control can arise from permissive parenting, which lacks firm boundaries and discipline. Conversely, families that demonstrate effective communication and conflict-resolution techniques can promote positive attitudes and actions.

Situational elements can also lead to unfavorable interactions and individual and societal issues. High-stress situations can intensify unfavorable feelings and actions due to external, professional, or personal pressures. For example, financial difficulties, job instability, and long-term illness can foster an environment that is conducive to negativity. For instance, the COVID-19 epidemic has dramatically raised stress levels over the world, which has exacerbated negativity in several ways, such as an increase in domestic violence, mental health problems, and societal unrest.

An intricate web that sustains negativity in interpersonal relationships is created by interacting with several historical, cultural, personal, and situational elements. A multidimensional strategy that considers these many dimensions is needed to combat negativity. Developing emotional intelligence and self-awareness on an individual level might assist people in identifying and controlling their negative inclinations. Acquiring proficient communication and conflict resolution abilities will lessen unfavorable encounters and encourage more favorable results.

Promoting inclusive and equitable workplaces can help society by lowering the structural elements that lead to negativity. Addressing power disparities and lowering discrimination can be facilitated by promoting diversity, equity, and inclusion in the workplace, schools, and communities. It is also possible to change society's attitudes in favor of more positivism by promoting candid communication and dispelling cultural narratives reinforcing prejudice and stereotypes.

In conclusion, many personal, societal, and environmental elements impact the historical and cultural settings that give rise to negativity. Knowing these roots and typical causes of unfavorable interactions can help one better appreciate how ubiquitous negativity is in human conduct. Negative interactions can be turned into learning opportunities, and more positive, harmonious relationships can be fostered by addressing these underlying causes and advocating for constructive solutions.

Psychological Factors

Human behavior and perception are greatly influenced by psychological elements, which frequently result in unfavorable acts and encounters. These include mental health conditions and cognitive biases, which have a major impact on how people perceive and react to their surroundings. This section examines the intricate connection between mental health conditions and harmful habits, as well as how cognitive biases affect perception and feed a vicious cycle of negativity.

A broad spectrum of psychological problems that impact mood, thought process, and behavior are included in mental health issues. An individual's conduct can be greatly influenced by conditions including depression, anxiety, bipolar illness, and personality disorders, which frequently result in unfavorable interactions and reactions. For instance, depression is typified by enduring melancholy, pessimism, and disinterest in or enjoyment from activities. Cognitive distortions such as overgeneralization, catastrophizing, and black-and-white thinking can occur in depressed people and lead to unfavorable perceptions of people and circumstances. Distorted thinking can result in conflict in personal and professional relationships, as well as disengagement and impatience.

Negative behaviors are also significantly influenced by anxiety disorders, which include social anxiety disorder, panic disorder, and generalized anxiety disorder. Anxiety disorders are frequently accompanied by excessive worry, fear, and physical symptoms like sweat and a fast heartbeat. These symptoms may include avoidance tendencies, impatience, and difficulty focusing, all of which may harm social interactions. An individual suffering from social anxiety disorder could steer clear of social gatherings, which can result in loneliness and make it difficult to establish connections. When pushed into social situations, they could appear distant or unwelcoming, leading to miscommunications and unfavorable opinions from others.

Negative behaviors can also arise from bipolar disorder, which is typified by severe mood fluctuations between mania and sadness. Manic episodes can cause people to act impulsively, become irritable, and become grandiose, which can strain relationships and cause arguments. On the other hand, depressed episodes can result in negativity, hopelessness, and withdrawal. Because of how erratic these mood swings can be, people may find it difficult to maintain consistent and constructive relationships with others, which can result in a vicious cycle of negativity and loneliness.

Personality disorders, including narcissistic personality disorder (NPD) and borderline personality disorder (BPD), provide additional examples of the link between mental health problems and harmful behaviors. Emotional dysregulation, fear of abandonment, and powerful emotions are common in people with borderline personality disorder (BPD). Impulsive actions, self-harm, and unstable relationships might result from these symptoms. BPD is often connected with persistent emotions of emptiness and rage, which can lead to bad interactions and disputes regularly. In a similar vein, people with NPD may display conceit, a deficiency of empathy, and a constant need for approval. These characteristics can contribute to a negative pattern by causing strained relationships, manipulative actions, and exploiting others.

Cognitive biases substantially impact how people perceive and understand their surroundings, which frequently results in bad actions and mental health difficulties. Cognitive biases are regular patterns of judgmental divergence from reality or reason, affecting perception and decision-making. These prejudices can warp a person's perception of reality, resulting in unfavorable assessments of circumstances and interactions.

The negativity bias is one type of bias that pertains to the inclination to prioritize bad information over positive information. This bias may cause people to discount or ignore the good parts of experiences, events, and feedback in favor of more emphasis on the bad. Consequently, people could become gloomy and see the negative side of neutral or ambiguous events. This increased emphasis on negativity can encourage negative behaviors like conflict, violence, and withdrawal when people become defensive in response to perceived threats or criticism.

Another cognitive bias is confirmation bias, which is the propensity to look for, analyze, and retain data that supports preexisting opinions and attitudes. Due to this bias, individuals may interpret interactions and situations in a way that promotes their pessimistic worldview, which can reinforce negative thoughts and impressions. For example, someone who thinks people are generally unreliable could pick out examples of betrayal or dishonesty and ignore proof of kindness and reliability. People who act by their distorted understanding of reality may exhibit negative behaviors due to this biased perspective, including distrust, hatred, and retreat.

Negative behaviors and perceptions are also significantly shaped by attribute-based biases. The fundamental attribution mistake is the inclination to ascribe one's conduct to external conditions and others' behavior to internal traits. Due to this bias, people may perceive the conduct of others as malicious and purposeful while justifying their bad behavior by citing contextual justifications. This can result in unfavorable judgments and interactions. In interpersonal relationships, this disparity in attribution may lead to miscommunications, disputes, and a lack of empathy.

Another attributional bias is the self-serving bias, which is the propensity to ascribe external influences to poor results and internal variables to positive ones. This prejudice can uphold one's self-worth while encouraging unfavorable interactions and behaviors. For instance, if someone denies involvement in a dispute, they can blame other people or outside events, implying a lack of accountability and resistance to alter unfavorable habits. This protective stance can obstruct communication and prolong a bad cycle in partnerships.

Negative interactions and behaviors are also influenced by stereotyping, a cognitive bias that entails applying generalizations about individual traits to large populations. Prejudice, discrimination, and unfavorable treatment of people due to their affiliation with a specific group can result from stereotypes. These skewed opinions may lead to unjust and aggressive interactions, which in turn may reinforce unfavorable acts and mindsets on both sides.

Negative behaviors and perceptions are influenced by a complicated web that is created by the interaction between mental health problems and cognitive biases. To tackle these problems, a multimodal strategy involving individual and societal interventions is needed. Individuals with mental health concerns can benefit from psychotherapy and counseling to improve emotional control, confront cognitive biases, and create healthy coping skills. It has been demonstrated that cognitive-behavioral therapy (CBT), in particular, is useful in treating cognitive biases and negative thought patterns, assisting people in gaining a more optimistic and balanced perspective.

Raising public knowledge and comprehension of mental health concerns can lessen stigma and foster compassion and support for individuals impacted. Programs for education and training can also assist people in identifying and reducing cognitive biases, promoting relationships and decision-making that are more equitable and logical. Reducing negative behaviors and encouraging positive relationships can also be achieved by establishing supportive environments that facilitate open communication and offer mental health resources.

In summary, psychological elements such as mental health conditions and cognitive biases are major contributors to unfavorable behaviors and views. Through skewed thinking and emotional dysregulation, mental health illnesses like depression, anxiety, bipolar disorder, and personality disorders can result in bad interactions. Negative attitudes and actions are made worse by cognitive biases such as confirmation, negativity, and attributional biases. To address these issues, it will be necessary for both individuals and society to raise awareness of mental health issues, offer efficient treatment, and lessen cognitive distortions, all of which will eventually lead to more productive and positive interactions.

Social Influences

Human behavior and interactions are greatly influenced by social factors, which frequently promote negativity in a variety of ways. Social dynamics, which include the interactions, procedures, and structures within societies and organizations, can foster the growth of unfavorable attitudes and behaviors. Furthermore, the ubiquitous impact of media and technology has revolutionized human communication and contact, frequently intensifying adverse relationships. This section investigates how media and technology promote negative interactions and how social dynamics lead to negativity.

Social dynamics is an essential component of human existence that molds how people interact in various social settings. Power, status, group norms, and social roles are some of the factors that shape these dynamics and can foster negative situations. For example, power disparities can result in confrontations and unfavorable interactions. Hierarchical organizational arrangements frequently lead to jealousy, power struggles, and rivalry between coworkers. It is possible for those in lower positions to feel oppressed or marginalized, which breeds hatred and resentment toward those in higher positions. On the other hand, people in authority often act authoritarian, which breeds suspicion and terror.

Negativity is also greatly aided by social hierarchies and status. People are frequently ranked according to various factors within any social group, including wealth, education, attractiveness, and social ties. These rankings can foster unpleasant emotions and actions by promoting feelings of superiority or inferiority. For instance, in school environments, pupils seen as popular or high achievers could bully or exclude others who are less well-liked or have academic difficulties. These unfavorable encounters can prolong cycles of negativity inside the group and cause long-term psychological harm.

Social roles and group norms also play a part in the dynamics of negativity. Groups frequently develop unwritten standards or norms that specify appropriate behavior. These norms can poison an atmosphere by encouraging bad habits like bullying, gossiping, and exclusion. Furthermore, people may feel pressured to engage in harmful activities to fit in or be accepted by society due to societal roles and expectations. For example, participating in risky activities like drug usage may be accepted as a sign of group commitment or as a rite of passage in some social circles. Even when such actions go against an individual's values or well-being, these forces can cause people to adopt and maintain harmful behaviors.

It is impossible to overstate the impact of media and technology on unfavorable interactions. The media and technology of the digital age have permeated every aspect of life, influencing communication, information access, and opinion formation. But in several other ways, these platforms can encourage and intensify harmful connections.

The media's presentation of bad behaviors and stereotypes is one of the main ways it spreads negativity. Because conflict, aggressiveness, and controversy tend to draw greater attention and involvement, these stories are frequently featured in news outlets, television shows, and motion pictures. People constantly exposed to unpleasant information may become less sensitive to aggressiveness and conflict, making such behaviors appear more normal or acceptable. Furthermore, biases and stereotypes are frequently reinforced by media portrayals, which serve to strengthen unfavorable opinions about particular populations. For example, the way that gender and race stereotypes are portrayed in the media can promote discrimination and prejudice, which in turn can lead to unfavorable encounters based on these biases.

Social media platforms have completely changed the way people communicate by allowing people to connect and exchange information instantly. Although these platforms have many advantages, they also create an environment conducive to unfavorable interactions. Online communication's anonymity and distance might lessen accountability by enabling people to act hostilely and voice disagreeable thoughts without worrying about the consequences. The online disinhibition effect is a phenomenon that can result in harassment, trolling, and cyberbullying. People may have serious psychological effects from these unfavorable encounters, including anxiety, depression, and, in severe cases, self-harm or suicide.

Negativity can also be influenced by social media platforms' algorithms and design. Content that receives a lot of interaction—including contentious or sensational posts—is frequently given priority by algorithms. As a result, there may be echo chambers where people are largely exposed to information that confirms their attitudes and beliefs. These can lead to polarizing views and unfavorable encounters. Negative behaviors and interactions can also be exacerbated by inadequacy, jealousy, and anger stemming from the pressure to present an idealized picture of oneself online and the need for social affirmation.

The workplace has changed due to technology, and these new dynamics may encourage negativity. The lines between work and home life have become hazier due to remote work and digital communication technologies, which have exacerbated stress and burnout. Lack of in-person engagement can lead to misconceptions and miscommunications, intensifying into confrontations and unfavorable encounters. Furthermore, the perpetual connectedness enabled by technology can foster a hypercompetitive atmosphere where workers experience pressure to constantly be present and perform at the best caliber, resulting in jealousy and hatred among coworkers.

A comprehensive strategy is needed to address how media, technology, and social dynamics contribute to negativity. Promoting knowledge and comprehension of these factors is essential from a societal perspective. A more critical and thoughtful attitude to the consumption and exchange of information can be fostered by education and training programs that assist people in identifying and challenging unfavorable social dynamics and media depictions.

Mitigating negativity also requires creating surroundings that are inclusive and supportive. Encouraging a workplace culture of empathy, respect, and cooperation can lessen rivalry, jealousy, and power struggles. By putting in place policies that support mental health and work-life balance, stress and burnout can be reduced, which lowers the possibility of unfavorable interactions. Promoting diversity and inclusivity in school environments can aid in upending status hierarchies and reduce bullying and other exclusionary behavior.

Reducing negativity can also be achieved through regulating media content and encouraging ethical journalism. The emphasis can be shifted from stories of conflict and violence to ones that are constructive and solution-focused by encouraging media outlets to prioritize fair and constructive reporting over sensationalism. A more inclusive and polite society can be promoted by encouraging diverse and truthful depictions in the media, which can help to dispel prejudices and preconceptions.

Increasing one's emotional intelligence and digital literacy can lessen the harmful effects of media and technology on a personal level. Programs for digital literacy can educate people on how to spot echo chambers, assess online content critically, and refrain from participating in or promoting unfavorable interactions. Through developing self-awareness, empathy, and effective communication skills, emotional intelligence training can lessen the probability of bad behaviors and foster positive relationships.

To sum up, social dynamics and the impact of media and technology are important factors that contribute to the spread of negativity. Social roles, group norms, status hierarchies, and power disparities can all foster an atmosphere conducive to developing bad attitudes and actions. These dynamics are amplified by media and technology, which prioritize sensational content, diminish responsibility, and perpetuate bad depictions. To address these influences, a comprehensive strategy that promotes awareness fosters supportive surroundings, controls media content, and develops digital literacy and emotional intelligence. More constructive and positive social interactions can be encouraged by recognizing and addressing the social variables contributing to negativity.

The Impact of Negativity

Over time, negativity may majorly impact relationships in both the personal and professional spheres and have profound and far-reaching impacts on both physical and mental health. Whether it originates from outside sources or personal experiences, negativity is ubiquitous and can harm interpersonal relationships and general well-being. Comprehending these effects is essential in formulating tactics to alleviate negativity and encourage positive connections.

Negativity emotionally can have a variety of negative effects. Chronic exposure to unfavorable beliefs, attitudes, or actions frequently makes people more stressed and anxious. The body's stress response systems can be triggered by ongoing stress from unfavorable interactions or surroundings, which raises cortisol and other stress hormone levels. Chronic activation can lead to emotional weariness, irritation, and a decreased ability to handle day-to-day difficulties. Prolonged negative thinking and stress can eventually lead to the emergence of mental health issues, including anxiety and depression. People who are exposed to unfavorable situations regularly may feel hopeless, have low self-esteem, and generally feel unsatisfied, which can exacerbate emotional distress.

The effects of negativity on physical health are similarly noteworthy. Prolonged negativity frequently results in chronic stress, which has been connected to several physical health problems. Long-term stress can impair immunity, leaving people more vulnerable to diseases and infections. Chronic illnesses like hypertension, cardiovascular disease, and gastrointestinal issues can also be facilitated by it. Negative behaviors, such as poor food choices, inactivity, and insufficient sleep, can increase health issues and exacerbate the physiological impacts of stress. People who are always stressed out, for instance, could turn to unhealthy coping strategies like binge eating, smoking, or drinking too much alcohol, all of which can be harmful to their physical well-being.

The enduring consequences of negativity on interpersonal relationships are extensive and complex. In relationships, negativity can foster a poisonous atmosphere that breeds resentment, miscommunication, and emotional distance. Persistent negativity can undermine trust and closeness in personal relationships involving family, friends, or love partners. For example, persistent criticism, blaming, or hate can cause a breakdown in mutual support and communication, making it challenging to settle disputes productively. The gradual deterioration of trust and closeness may give rise to emotions of loneliness and discontent, which may ultimately culminate in the breakup of partnerships.

Anger can be especially harmful in love relationships. Relationship satisfaction and emotional connection may deteriorate in couples who frequently engage in unpleasant behaviors like disputes, defensiveness, or contempt. When negativity permeates a relationship, it can create a vicious cycle of blame and resentment, making it difficult for partners to resolve conflicts and keep a positive, supporting bond. According to research, partnerships with high levels of negativity are more likely to end in divorce because it may become harder for partners to maintain the emotional commitment required for a happy and lasting relationship.

Negativity also has a major effect on work relationships. Negativity can lead to a toxic workplace with low morale, low productivity, and high turnover rates. Employee motivation and job satisfaction may suffer if they are subjected to unfavorable workplace practices like micromanagement, unjustified criticism, or bullying. Stress and discontent that follow can hurt team dynamics and organizational effectiveness by raising absenteeism and performance levels.

Workplace connections can be weakened by unfavorable interactions, which also makes cooperation and teamwork more challenging. It could be difficult for staff members who participate in bad behaviors or see them develop rapport and trust with their peers. This mistrust can obstruct productive dialogue and teamwork, resulting in inefficiencies and disputes. Negative relationships might lead to a shattered workplace where staff members feel abandoned and disengaged.

Furthermore, negativity can have a significant negative effect on career growth. Negative or uncooperative employees may have a lower chance of being promoted or receiving recognition since their actions could be viewed as harmful to the organization's performance and the team's cohesiveness. Detrimental workplace practices can, therefore, have a long-term damaging impact on prospects for professional progress and lead to a stalled career trajectory.

A broad approach is needed to address the negative effects of negativity on relationships in both personal and professional spheres and mental and physical health. Individuals can lessen the impact of negativity by learning stress management techniques and cultivating optimistic thinking. Reducing the detrimental effects of negative thoughts and behaviors on emotional well-being can be accomplished through strategies including stress management, cognitive restructuring, and mindfulness.

Reducing the negative impact of negativity on one's physical health can also be achieved by prioritizing sleep, eating a balanced diet, and exercising frequently.

Promoting honest and helpful communication in interpersonal relationships can aid in addressing and resolving unpleasant exchanges. Relationship counseling or therapy can help families and couples by giving them the skills and techniques to manage conflict, communicate better, and reestablish trust. Relationships can be strengthened, and negative consequences mitigated by laying a foundation of understanding and support for one another.

A positive and encouraging environment must be established to lessen the effects of negativity at work. Respect, cooperation, and constructive criticism are all things that organizations may foster with the use of policies and procedures. A more upbeat and effective work atmosphere can also be achieved by offering chances for professional growth and supporting a good work-life balance. Training courses that concentrate on stress management, emotional intelligence, and conflict resolution can assist staff members in gaining the abilities needed to handle difficult situations.

In conclusion, negativity has a significant and varied effect on relationships in both personal and professional spheres and mental and physical health. Long-term negative exposure can cause physical health issues, mental suffering, and a breakdown in interpersonal connections. A comprehensive strategy incorporating personalized stress management techniques, encouraging constructive communication in interpersonal interactions, and establishing supportive work environments is needed to address these effects. Individuals and organizations can promote healthier and more pleasant connections by identifying and mitigating the impact of negativity, ultimately improving overall well-being and relationship satisfaction.

Recognizing Negativity

A lot of things in our lives can be impacted by negativity, which can change how we relate to each other and ourselves. It's critical to identify and deal with harmful tendencies if you want to promote healthier relationships and enhance your general well-being. This section dives into understanding the underlying roots of negativity to better address and minimize its consequences. It also covers how to recognize negative tendencies in oneself and others.

Self-awareness is the first step towards recognizing undesirable patterns in oneself. Recognizing when and how negativity appears in one's thoughts, acts, and interactions requires self-reflection, an essential skill. Consistent, recurring motifs in our reactions to obstacles and social encounters frequently indicate negative patterns. For instance, someone who routinely criticizes themselves could have a habit of negative self-talk in which they constantly cast doubt on their abilities and accomplishments. This trend may indicate deeper problems like perfectionism or low self-esteem. It's important to focus on the language used in self-reflection and the regularity with which negative ideas surface to identify these patterns.

Pessimism is another typical negative pattern in which a person expects the worse in various situations. This thinking can result in a self-fulfilling prophecy, in which unfavorable expectations cause conduct to take on predictable bad outcomes. For example, a person who expects to fail at a job interview can be unconfident when they go in, which could hurt their performance and confirm their conviction that they will fail. Finding these patterns entails examining how a person's attitude in life influences their behavior and interactions.

Behavioral responses are another way that negative patterns appear. For instance, a pattern of emotional dysregulation may be revealed by a consistent outburst of rage or irritation during stressful situations. Frequent outbursts, a propensity to place blame, or an incapacity to properly handle stress could indicate this pattern. Acknowledging these activities necessitates a sincere evaluation of one's responses and how they affect interpersonal relationships. Mindfulness and cognitive restructuring are two emotional control techniques that can be useful in addressing these habits and encouraging better reactions.

Recognizing harmful tendencies in other people requires acute observation and compassionate comprehension. When someone is acting negatively, it can show up as constant criticism, hate, or a general feeling of unhappiness. For example, a coworker who regularly finds fault with others' work could display a pattern of negativity that lowers team morale and reduces productivity. It takes awareness of how other people's actions affect relationships and group dynamics to spot these patterns. Considering any potential underlying concerns that might be causing these bad actions, it's also critical to treat these observations with empathy.

To properly address and mitigate the impacts of negativity, one must thoroughly understand its underlying origins. The underlying reasons for negativity can be intricate and multidimensional, frequently combining social, psychological, and environmental elements. Negative patterns can be greatly influenced by psychological factors such as unresolved trauma, ongoing stress, and mental health problems. People who have gone through trauma in the past, for instance, could adopt unhealthy coping strategies and behavioral patterns that mirror their unhealed emotional wounds. Examining a person's past and seeing how experiences from the past may have shaped their present behavior are necessary steps in identifying these underlying causes.

Negativity is also significantly influenced by long-term stress. Stressful life circumstances, such as money troubles, marital issues, or pressures from the workplace, can cause bad thoughts and actions. Prolonged stress can trigger the body's stress reaction mechanisms, resulting in agitation, nervousness, and emotional depletion. Examining the origins and effects of stressors in a person's life is necessary to comprehend how stress contributes to negativity. Stress management strategies, such as time management, relaxation training, and seeking support, can lessen long-term stress's harmful patterns and effects.

Negativity can also be a core cause of mental health conditions, including depression and anxiety. Persistent feelings of melancholy, pessimism, and low self-worth are common characteristics of depression. These symptoms might include negative self-talk and social disengagement. Excessive concern and fear brought on by anxiety can lead to pessimistic attitudes and avoidance tendencies. To treat these mental health conditions, getting help from a professional—such as counseling or medication—is necessary to control symptoms and enhance emotional stability.

Environmental and social variables are also important in cultivating negativity. Negative attitudes and behaviors can thrive in social contexts of rivalry, conflict, or a lack of support. For instance, a workplace culture that prioritizes competition over collaboration could result in unfavorable interactions among coworkers, such as undermining and gossiping. Similar to this, individuals may develop bad tendencies as a result of conflictual or critical home settings. Recognizing the areas that may require assistance and modification and evaluating the larger context in which harmful behaviors occur are crucial steps in comprehending the impact of social and environmental factors.

A person's principles and beliefs can sometimes fuel negativity. For instance, people with inflexible ideas about what constitutes success and failure could be more prone to low self-esteem and feelings of inadequacy. Examining one's values and beliefs can reveal how internalized ideas affect behavior and contribute to harmful behaviors. Reframing and challenging limiting beliefs might lessen negativity and encourage a more impartial viewpoint.

An all-encompassing strategy that incorporates proactive tactics, empathy, and self-awareness is needed to combat negativity. Techniques like stress management, mindfulness, and cognitive-behavioral therapy (CBT) can be helpful resources for people who want to change their harmful tendencies. While CBT focuses on confronting and altering negative thinking patterns, mindfulness helps develop self-awareness and acceptance of unpleasant thoughts. Stress management approaches can support emotional resilience and lessen the negative effects of ongoing stress.

Fostering open communication and providing support can be useful tactics for people dealing with negativity in others. Addressing underlying problems and reducing harmful behaviors can be facilitated by promoting an atmosphere where people feel heard and understood. More adaptable actions and attitudes can also be promoted by offering constructive criticism and encouraging positive reinforcement. Sympathetic listening and support can aid healthy relationships and the change process.

In summary, detecting negative patterns in oneself and others and comprehending the underlying causes of these patterns is essential to recognizing and resolving negativity. Self-awareness, empathy, and observation are crucial when determining the root reasons for undesirable behaviors. Chronic stress, mental health conditions, psychological problems, and social and environmental elements can all be considered root causes of negativity. A complex strategy that includes proactive tactics, self-awareness, and compassionate support is needed to combat negativity. By comprehending and tackling the elements that lead to negativity, people can cultivate more positive relationships and enhance their general well-being.

CHAPTER II

Self-Awareness and Emotional Intelligence

The Importance of Self-Awareness

A key component of emotional intelligence and personal development, self-awareness forms the basis for satisfying relationships and a happy existence. It entails being able to look within and comprehend one's ideas, feelings, and actions, as well as how they impact and are impacted by the outside world. There are several areas in which self-awareness is important, such as career achievement, interpersonal connections, and personal growth. This section explores the significance of self-awareness, highlighting its advantages, difficulties, and methods for developing this vital quality.

Fundamentally, self-awareness is people's capacity to comprehend better their inner states—their feelings, motives, and values. This knowledge is essential for personal growth, enabling people to identify their advantages and disadvantages. People aware of their strengths can use these qualities to further their aims and gain confidence. On the other hand, acknowledging their shortcomings presents a chance for development and enhancement. For instance, someone conscious of their propensity to put things off can proactively combat this behavior by making clearer goals or looking for time management techniques. Self-awareness enables people to make well-informed decisions and leads them to live more purposefully and clearly in their personal and professional lives.

Emotional intelligence heavily depends on self-awareness, which includes the capacity to identify, comprehend, and regulate one's emotions and those of others. Effective relationship management and communication require emotional intelligence. Self-aware people can better understand their emotional reactions and how those affect how they interact with others. For example, people aware of their emotional patterns and triggers can better control their reactions when faced with conflict or stressful circumstances. This self-control promotes more positive communication and helps stop emotional outbursts. Furthermore, self-awareness improves interpersonal interactions and promotes mutual understanding by allowing people to identify and validate their own emotional experiences, which helps them sympathize with others.

It is equally important to be self-aware in professional settings. It helps people succeed in their careers by improving their teamwork, flexibility, and leadership abilities. Self-conscious leaders are better able to manage their teams because they are aware of their leadership style and how it affects others. They may also modify their strategy to suit the needs of their team and are more receptive to criticism. For example, a self-aware leader may realize that some team members find their direct communication style harsh and modify their manner to promote a more cooperative environment. Setting reasonable job objectives and coordinating one's professional ambitions with one's values and strengths are two more benefits of self-awareness. This alignment ensures greater job satisfaction and contentment as people select jobs authentically aligned with their identities.

Self-awareness has numerous advantages but can be challenging to cultivate and sustain. It necessitates being prepared to face difficult facts and continue introspection. It can be challenging for many people to examine their ideas, feelings, and behaviors objectively as part of becoming self-aware. This self-examination may uncover facets of oneself that are challenging to acknowledge or alter, including ingrained fears or ingrained behavioral patterns. One must be resilient and dedicated to personal development to overcome these obstacles. Self-awareness can be developed by engaging in writing, mindfulness meditation, or asking trustworthy people for feedback. These activities can help one become more self-aware by offering insights and encouraging a non-judgmental mindset.

For example, mindfulness meditation is an effective method of increasing self-awareness. It entails focusing on the here and now and objectively evaluating one's thoughts and emotions without bias. Through this exercise, people can better comprehend their habitual responses and become more aware of their interior feelings. Frequent mindfulness can result in better focus, better emotional control, and a deeper inner serenity. Similarly, journaling offers a disciplined method of reflecting on one's experiences, feelings, and objectives. People can better understand their behavior patterns and make more educated judgments on their personal development by journaling their thoughts and feelings.

Getting input from others is a useful tactic for improving self-awareness. Reliable friends, relatives, or coworkers can offer insightful viewpoints on one's actions and how they affect others. Individuals who receive constructive comments can better identify areas for growth and blind spots that may not be visible through self-reflection alone. But facing criticism with an open mind and a desire to pick up new skills is crucial. It is better to see constructive criticism as a chance for improvement than a personal jab. Positively accepting criticism can help you make significant progress and build deeper bonds with others.

Apart from influencing one's personal and professional spheres, self-awareness also plays a role in one's general welfare and contentment with life. Those who are aware of their wants, values, and desires are better able to make decisions that are true to who they are. This alignment fosters a sense of purpose and contentment as people pursue relationships and objectives consistent with their basic values. A person who values creativity could look for chances to express themselves artistically or pursue a career in the creative industry, increasing their sense of fulfillment and success. Self-awareness strengthens resilience because self-conscious people can better deal with life's obstacles since they are aware of their coping strategies and strengths.

In addition, self-awareness is essential for problem-solving and conflict resolution. People who possess self-awareness can view problems more objectively, acknowledging their roles in the matter and comprehending how their feelings and actions influence the circumstances. Being self-aware enables people to communicate and solve problems more effectively because they can articulate their demands and concerns clearly and respectfully while also being open to hearing other people's viewpoints. People can improve their relationships and strive toward win-win solutions by confronting problems with self-awareness.

To sum up, self-awareness is a vital quality that greatly influences emotional intelligence, professional success, personal development, and general well-being. It entails developing a greater awareness of one's ideas, feelings, and actions and realizing how these aspects affect communication and choice-making. While growing in self-awareness can be difficult at times—such as when facing hard facts and reflecting on oneself—it also has many advantages, such as better emotional control, stronger bonds with others, and a higher quality of life. Techniques like writing, asking for feedback, and practicing mindfulness meditation can help people become more self-aware and promote personal development. Through developing self-awareness, people can live more purposefully, resiliently, and with better clarity, eventually resulting in a more happy and meaningful life.

Emotional Intelligence Basics

A vital component of human functioning, emotional intelligence (EI), greatly impacts both personal and professional performance. It includes the capacity to identify, comprehend, and control one's own emotions and the capacity to identify and affect the feelings of others. While problem-solving and logical thinking were the primary cognitive skills used to measure intelligence in the past, current knowledge recognizes the critical role emotional intelligence plays in success and well-being. This section offers a thorough analysis of the fundamentals of emotional intelligence, outlining its main elements, significance, and development techniques.

Emotional intelligence is fundamentally a set of abilities that help people successfully traverse challenging social situations. Daniel Goleman popularized "emotional intelligence" in the mid-1990s and highlighted five essential components: motivation, self-regulation, empathy, self-awareness, and social skills. Each element plays a part in a person's capacity to regulate their emotional terrain and engage in harmonious interactions with others. The capacity to identify and comprehend one's feelings and how they influence one's ideas and actions is known as self-awareness. It entails candidly assessing one's advantages and disadvantages and thoroughly understanding how emotions affect behavior. Since self-awareness enables people to make educated judgments and understand how their feelings impact their interactions with others, it is fundamental to emotional intelligence.

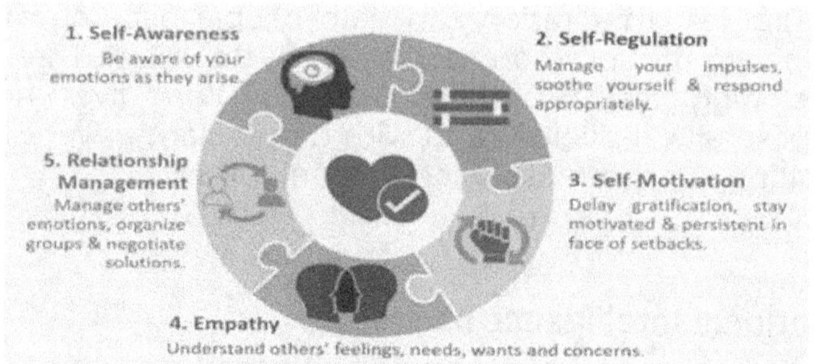

The capacity to constructively regulate one's emotions is known as self-regulation. It entails restraint of urges, composure under duress, and flexibility in response to shifting conditions. Maintaining a balanced emotional state is essential for making deliberate decisions and upholding good relationships, and it can be achieved through effective self-regulation. For example, someone who can control their anger during a heated debate is likelier to have a productive conversation instead of intensifying the argument. Being resilient and focused on adversity is another aspect of self-regulation that promotes achievement and general well-being.

Another essential element of emotional intelligence is motivation. It entails having the will to succeed and the capacity to keep going in the face of difficulties. People with high emotional intelligence are generally intrinsically motivated, meaning they are motivated more by inner fulfillment and happiness than by material or social benefits. Strong dedication and a sense of purpose are fostered by this internal motivation, which increases resilience and the capacity to overcome challenges. Motivated people are more likely to establish and work toward important goals and to keep going when things get tough.

The ability to comprehend and experience another person's emotions is known as empathy. It entails being sensitive to the feelings and viewpoints of others and reacting accordingly. Empathy allows people to connect with others emotionally and effectively meet their needs, which is crucial for establishing and preserving healthy relationships. An empathic manager may better address the problems of their team members and foster a positive work atmosphere. Since empathy fosters an appreciation for diverse perspectives and the pursuit of win-win solutions, it also plays a role in effective communication and conflict resolution.

Various competencies that support productive interactions and connections with others are included in the social skills category. These abilities include leadership, teamwork, communication, and dispute resolution. People with great social skills are skilled at establishing rapport, influencing others favorably, and navigating social situations. They can effectively manage interpersonal dynamics, constructively settle disputes, and motivate and guide others. A team leader possessing exceptional social skills, for instance, can cultivate a cooperative and efficient work atmosphere through skillfully conveying expectations, resolving problems, and inspiring team members.

Emotional intelligence is important for more than just successful interactions at work. Studies have indicated a strong correlation between mental health, general well-being, and emotional intelligence. High emotional intelligence people can better manage stress, preserve wholesome relationships, and accomplish personal and professional objectives. Positive feelings like contentment and satisfaction are more common, and they tend to feel more confident. Additionally, emotional intelligence improves physical health by lowering stress and encouraging healthy behaviors.

It takes practice, criticism, and self-reflection to build emotional intelligence. Raising self-awareness is one of the first stages of developing emotional intelligence. This can be accomplished by engaging in activities like journaling, mindfulness, and asking for input from others. By practicing mindfulness, people can become more aware of their emotional states and learn to examine their thoughts and feelings without passing judgment. Keeping a journal offers a disciplined approach to consider one's emotional encounters and tendencies. Getting input from reliable people can provide insightful knowledge about how one's actions and feelings affect others.

Techniques including mood control, cognitive restructuring, and stress management can help with self-regulation. People who use stress management strategies, like time management and relaxation exercises, can lessen the effects of stress and preserve their emotional equilibrium. Cognitive restructuring is recognizing, questioning, and substituting harmful thought patterns with positive ones. Deep breathing and mindfulness are two examples of emotion management techniques that can assist people in controlling their emotional reactions and preserving composure.

A growth mentality, emphasis on intrinsic rewards, and establishing specific, attainable goals are all effective ways to promote motivation. Individuals can maintain their motivation by focusing on inherent rewards and setting clear, quantifiable goals that give them a sense of purpose and direction. Adopting a growth mindset entails viewing obstacles as chances for learning and development rather than as dangers to one's self-worth. This thinking motivates people to keep pursuing their goals and see failures as chances to improve.

Active listening, considering other people's perspectives, and engaging in acts of kindness can all improve empathy. Fully interacting with others and comprehending their viewpoints while avoiding interruptions or presumptions is known as active listening. Placing oneself in another person's shoes and considering their feelings and points of view is known as perspective-taking. Being compassionate is being nice and understanding of other people's needs. By engaging in these activities, people can strengthen their relationships with others and become more adept at reacting sympathetically to various circumstances.

Effective teamwork, communication, and conflict-resolution strategies can help build social skills. It takes both careful listening and clear expression of oneself to communicate effectively. Cooperation entails appreciating different viewpoints and striving toward shared objectives. Techniques for resolving conflicts, such as mediation and negotiation, assist people in approaching disputes positively and coming up with compromises. Gaining these abilities improves communication between people and fosters a supportive and constructive social environment.

To sum up, emotional intelligence is an essential quality that affects relationships that work, general well-being, and success in both the personal and professional spheres. It includes self-awareness, motivation, self-regulation, empathy, and social skills, all of which help people navigate their emotional terrain and engage in harmonious interactions with others. Self-reflection, practice, and feedback are all important components of developing emotional intelligence, which focuses on boosting motivation, controlling emotions, cultivating self-awareness, and advancing social skills. People can improve their relationships, better understand themselves, and live better lives overall by developing their emotional intelligence.

Developing Empathy
The capacity for empathy, or the understanding and sharing of another person's emotions, is an essential part

of emotional intelligence and a prerequisite for developing deep connections. It entails not just identifying the feelings of another individual but also connecting with their experiences and reacting suitably. Developing empathy depends on fostering compassionate connections, improving communication, and advancing social harmony. The significance of empathy, methods for cultivating it, and its effects on interpersonal and professional relationships are all covered in this section.

The importance of empathy is felt in many facets of interpersonal communication. It is the cornerstone of clear communication and comprehension, enabling people to connect more deeply. Interactions are more likely to be sincere and encouraging when empathy is present, which builds stronger bonds and a more unified social environment. People with empathy can better negotiate tricky social situations and resolve disputes positively. They can close gaps in knowledge, attend to the needs of others, and create a welcoming environment.

The first step towards developing empathy is to practice active listening. Engaging fully in another person's speech, both verbally and nonverbally, while avoiding interruptions and passing judgment, is known as active listening. It necessitates paying close attention to the speaker's words, voice tone, and body language. By concentrating on these aspects, people can better comprehend the speaker's emotional state and underlying problems. By actively listening, you can show the speaker you appreciate and acknowledge their experiences. Establishing rapport and trust through this method paves the way for sympathetic reactions.

Perspective-taking is another essential skill for the development of empathy. They are putting oneself in another person's shoes and thinking about one's possible feelings or reactions, known as perspective-taking.

Through this mental activity, people can develop a broader appreciation for other people's perspectives and experiences. Various activities, including reading widely-ranging works of literature, conversing with individuals from diverse backgrounds, and participating in role-playing games, can promote the development of perspective-taking. People can better understand the range of human experiences and emotions by exposing themselves to diverse viewpoints.

Additionally, self-awareness and emotional control can foster empathy. Developing empathy requires understanding one's own emotions and how they affect others. People aware of their emotional states can more identify and relate to others experiencing similar feelings. For instance, someone who has gone through sadness might be more understanding of another person's suffering and more qualified to provide support. Maintaining a balanced viewpoint and controlling one's emotional reactions are components of emotional management. People who possess this self-awareness are better able to react to the emotions of others without becoming overtaken by their feelings and with sensitivity.

Compassion practice is another powerful method for cultivating empathy. Understanding another person's feelings and acting to lessen their pain are components of compassion. It necessitates taking the initiative to support and attend to the needs of others. Volunteering for nonprofit organizations or offering emotional support to a friend during a trying period are compassionate activities. People can strengthen their capacity for empathy and constructively contribute to a community by acting compassionately. In addition to promoting unity and common humanity, compassion highlights the value of empathy in developing enduring connections.

Exposure to many situations and experiences might improve empathy even more. Interacting with others from diverse cultural, financial, or social backgrounds enhances comprehension of various life encounters and obstacles. This exposure promotes a more accepting and compassionate way of thinking by dispelling myths and preconceptions. Engaging in community work, travel, or cross-cultural exchange initiatives can yield significant insights into the lives of others and foster a heightened understanding of varied viewpoints. People can get a more complex and compassionate view of the world by immersing themselves in various settings.

Overcoming obstacles to empathic involvement is another aspect of developing empathy. These obstacles can be emotional hurdles, preconceived notions, or personal biases that make interacting with others difficult. For instance, preexisting conceptions about a specific group of individuals might impair empathy and impair judgment. Self-reflection and a dedication to confronting and conquering these prejudices are necessary for addressing them. It entails actively searching out opposing views, challenging preconceived notions, and evaluating one's assumptions. By facing these obstacles, people can cultivate a more genuine and compassionate approach to social interactions.

Developing empathy has a significant and wide-ranging effect. Empathy promotes stronger bonding, improved communication, and deeper connections in interpersonal relationships. It enables people to handle disagreements with more empathy and understanding, which supports more successful settlement and reconciliation. Additionally, empathic people are more inclined to offer their loved ones emotional support and encouragement, which improves their general well-being. Empathy enhances customer interactions, teamwork, and leadership in work environments. Employees who practice empathy foster a healthy and cooperative work environment, and leaders who exhibit empathy are better equipped to inspire and motivate their teams.

Understanding and meeting customers' requirements can result in higher satisfaction and loyalty, another area in which empathy is essential in customer service.

To sum up, cultivating empathy is critical to creating meaningful connections, efficient communication, and a society that values compassion. It entails techniques like perspective-taking, active listening, emotional control, and compassion. Deeper connections with people can be made possible by overcoming obstacles to empathy and being exposed to various situations. Empathy has advantages in both the personal and professional spheres, strengthening bonds between people, fostering better teamwork, and building a more encouraging community. People can become more empathetic, have better relationships, become more emotionally intelligent, and make the world more peaceful and compassionate by practicing empathy.

Managing Your Emotions

The ability to control one's emotions is essential for preserving one's well-being and succeeding in various spheres of life. Even though emotions are a necessary part of being human, they can occasionally become overwhelming or disturbing if they are not controlled. Establishing and maintaining healthy relationships, making wise decisions, and accomplishing long-term objectives depend on an individual's ability to control and navigate their emotional terrain. This section examines the value of controlling one's emotions, techniques for doing so, and how successful emotion control affects one's overall quality of life.

One cannot stress how crucial it is to control one's emotions. Our emotions influence our thoughts, actions, and social relationships. Ineffective emotion management can result in rash decisions, miscommunications, and confrontations. For instance, uncontrolled rage may lead to heated disputes or terrible choices, while ongoing anxiety can make it difficult to concentrate and work efficiently. However, people who can control their emotions well can react to events in a calculated and deliberate way. It is all possible by better decision-making, enhanced interpersonal interactions, and a more balanced attitude to life's obstacles. People can improve their overall contentment, resilience, and mental health by learning how to control their emotions.

Self-awareness is a key tactic for handling emotions. Being self-conscious entails being aware of one's feelings and how they affect one's actions. Since it enables people to recognize patterns and triggers in their emotional reactions, this awareness is the first step toward emotional regulation. Self-awareness can be developed with the help of practices like writing and mindfulness. Engaging in mindfulness entails observing one's thoughts and emotions in the here and now without judgment. People who engage in this exercise improve their awareness of their emotional states and gain an understanding of their reactions. Keeping a journal offers a systematic approach to considering everyday emotional encounters, recognizing trends, and comprehending the fundamental reasons behind feelings. More self-aware people can control their emotions more effectively and make wiser decisions.

Emotional regulation is a key tactic for handling emotions. Controlling and modifying one's emotional reactions to suit the needs of a given circumstance is known as emotional regulation. It includes a range of methods and approaches that support people in efficiently controlling their emotions. Cognitive restructuring is one such method that modifies unfavorable thought patterns to affect emotional reactions. Reframing a difficult activity as a chance for progress instead of a threat is one example of cognitive restructuring that may be used when someone feels overwhelmed. This change in viewpoint can boost motivation and lessen worry.

Other useful techniques for managing emotions include deep breathing and relaxation techniques. Deep breathing exercises aim to lessen physiological signs of stress and soothe the nervous system by concentrating on deep, deliberate breaths. People can relax their muscles, reduce their heart rate, and improve their emotional regulation skills by practicing deep breathing. Similarly, by encouraging both physical and mental relaxation, progressive muscle relaxation and guided imagery can assist people in managing their stress and anxiety.

The creation of coping mechanisms is a crucial component of emotional regulation. Coping strategies are ways to deal with stress and bad feelings and lessen their effects. Different people have different effective coping mechanisms, including exercise, hobbies, or social support. For example, research has demonstrated that physical activity can lessen the symptoms of depression and anxiety by enhancing mood and generating endorphins. Hobbies and leisure pursuits can give people a constructive way to release tension and provide them fulfillment and happiness. Social support—talking to friends or getting professional counseling—can offer practical help and emotional comfort during trying times.

Developing resilience is yet another essential part of emotional regulation. Resilience is the capacity to overcome hardship and keep a positive attitude in the face of setbacks. Building a mindset that views setbacks as chances for improvement and education is essential to becoming resilient. Developing problem-solving abilities, keeping an optimistic outlook, and setting reasonable goals are all techniques for fostering resilience. For instance, people who perceive obstacles as transient and manageable are more inclined to persist and overcome challenges. People can better control their emotional reactions to stress and keep their motivation and hope by developing resilience.

Recognizing and addressing the underlying causes of emotions is another essential component of effective emotion regulation. Emotions frequently result from underlying ideas, convictions, or encounters. Understanding the underlying causes of specific emotions and how to regulate them better can be gained by locating and resolving them. For example, if someone always feels inadequate, it could be beneficial to investigate the underlying assumptions or experiences causing these sentiments. People can work toward resolving fundamental difficulties and lessening the severity of negative feelings by addressing these root causes.

Effective emotion management affects many facets of life, such as successful career relationships and interpersonal interactions. Emotional control in interpersonal relationships improves empathy, communication, and conflict resolution. Emotional control increases a person's capacity for productive conversation, clear communication, and understanding and compassionate interactions. As people can handle disagreements and difficulties better, relationships become healthier and more satisfying.

Emotional intelligence is essential to preserving professionalism, output, and job happiness in the workplace. Emotional control enables people to deal with stress at work, adjust to changes, and communicate with coworkers and clients productively. A manager who can control their anxiety and emotions, for instance, is better able to lead their team, give helpful criticism, and resolve disagreements at work. Likewise, workers who control their emotions are more likely to function well under duress, uphold a positive working rapport with colleagues, and foster a cooperative and fruitful work environment.

Gaining emotional control is a lifelong process that calls for constant effort and introspection. It entails realizing that emotions are dynamic and modifying tactics as necessary. People may face various emotional difficulties throughout their lives, and developing new skills and being open to learning are essential for good emotional management. Self-care, requesting assistance, and constant improvement of emotional regulation skills can assist people in navigating the intricacies of their emotional terrain and preserving general well-being.

To sum up, effective emotion management is an essential ability that affects relationships, career performance, and personal well-being. It entails coping mechanisms, self-awareness, emotional control, resilience, and tackling the underlying causes of emotions. Good emotion control makes it possible for people to react to circumstances in a measured and considered way, enhancing decision-making, fostering better relationships, and increasing happiness. People can better handle life's obstacles, keep emotional equilibrium, and accomplish their goals by honing their emotional management abilities. Effective emotion management is a journey that requires constant introspection and adjustment, but the rewards are significant and wide-ranging.

Personal Growth and Emotional Resilience

To lead a happy and balanced life, personal development and emotional resilience are intertwined ideas. Emotional resilience is the capacity to cope with and overcome hardship, stress, and emotional difficulties, whereas personal growth is the ongoing process of self-improvement, self-awareness, and development. Combined, these ideas help people deal with life's challenges more effectively and with greater ease. This section examines the connection between emotional resilience and personal development and methods for promoting both and their effects on success and general well-being.

Personal growth is known as a person's continuous path of self-improvement and self-discovery that touches on many aspects of their life. It entails establishing and working toward objectives, improving abilities, and deepening one's awareness of the self and the outside environment. The driving forces behind personal progress are the passion for meaningful objectives and self-improvement. It necessitates a readiness to venture outside one's comfort zone, welcome novel encounters, and draw lessons from achievements and setbacks. People can improve their general quality of life, get a stronger sense of purpose, and boost their self-confidence by engaging in personal growth.

Conversely, emotional resilience is the ability to endure and bounce back from emotional hardship and misfortune. It entails keeping an optimistic attitude, adjusting to difficult circumstances, and controlling one's emotional reactions. Being resilient means facing challenges head-on with fortitude and adaptability rather than trying to avoid them. It helps people deal with stress, recover from setbacks, and progress despite difficulties. A vital element of human development is emotional resilience, which offers the groundwork for conquering obstacles and pursuing self-improvement.

Personal development and emotional toughness are mutually beneficial. Overcoming and overcoming obstacles is a common part of personal development, and it can test and strengthen emotional resilience. On the other hand, emotional resilience promotes personal development by giving one the emotional fortitude required to keep going after objectives despite setbacks. For instance, someone looking to progress in their career may encounter roadblocks like job rejections or setbacks. Their capacity for resilience in the face of adversity enables them to draw lessons from the past, modify their approach, and keep pursuing their professional objectives. Personal development and emotional toughness feed off one another to create a cycle of ongoing adaptation and growth.

Setting goals, using coping mechanisms, and cultivating self-awareness are all necessary for emotional growth and resilience. Since self-awareness entails knowing one's strengths, shortcomings, values, and aspirations, it is the cornerstone of personal progress. Through introspection and self-reflection, people can learn more about their goals, motivations, and areas where they can grow. Self-awareness enables people to make wise decisions regarding their growth, match their behaviors with their values, and set meaningful and attainable goals. Additionally, it promotes increased resilience and flexibility by assisting people in identifying and resolving emotional difficulties.

Setting goals is yet another essential component of resilience and personal development. Establishing precise, measurable goals gives people focus and inspiration to develop themselves on their initiative. Setting SMART goals—specific, measurable, achievable, relevant, and time-bound—is necessary for effective goal-setting. Larger objectives can be broken down into more achievable segments so that people can monitor their progress and stay motivated. Setting goals also helps people learn new things, gain more information, and overcome challenges—all supporting resilience and personal development.

The development of resilience and the management of emotional stress both require coping mechanisms. Different coping mechanisms can guide people through difficult circumstances and preserve emotional equilibrium. For instance, problem-solving strategies entail determining answers to particular issues and implementing workable solutions. This proactive strategy can boost one's sense of control and lessen powerlessness. Emotion-focused coping also includes controlling emotional reactions to stress through mindfulness exercises, relaxation methods, or social support-seeking. These techniques support people in preserving their emotional equilibrium and developing their resilience in the face of difficulty.

Fostering a growth attitude is a crucial part of building emotional resilience. Believing that skills and intelligence can be developed via work, education, and perseverance is known as having a growth mindset. People with a growth mentality see setbacks as chances for personal development rather than insurmountable roadblocks. This way of thinking inspires people to seize learning opportunities, persevere through challenges, and never stop trying to better themselves. Developing a growth mindset can help people become more resilient by encouraging them to see failures and setbacks as chances for growth and improvement.

Self-care routines are crucial for emotional fortitude and personal development. Taking intentional steps to preserve one's physical, mental, and emotional well-being is known as self-care. Physical self-care fundamentals include getting enough sleep, eating a balanced diet, and exercising regularly. Engaging in hobbies, practicing mindfulness, and pursuing social relationships are mental and emotional self-care examples. Self-care promotes resilience and personal growth by assisting people in managing stress, preserving emotional equilibrium, and improving general well-being.

Another important aspect of developing emotional resilience is creating a network of supportive social connections. People who receive social assistance feel connected, understood, and encouraged when things are tough. Support groups, friends, family, and mentors can provide insightful viewpoints, practical help, and emotional support. Developing and maintaining relationships with encouraging people helps boost resilience since they can be a dependable source of solace and direction. Furthermore, assisting others can strengthen one's sense of grit and personal development by establishing a mutually beneficial support network.

Relationships with others, achieving professional success, and general well-being are just a few of the domains in which personal development and emotional resilience have an impact. People who place a high value on their growth and resilience are more likely to interact meaningfully and encouragingly with others in their relationships. They can resolve disputes with more compassion and understanding, improve their relationships, and forge closer bonds. In the workplace, resilience and personal development are essential for meeting objectives, adjusting to changes, and conquering obstacles. People who possess resilience are likelier to stick with their jobs, look for chances to grow, and be upbeat in the face of adversity.

Personal development and emotional resilience have a major impact on overall well-being. Emotional stability, self-worth, and life pleasure are higher in those pursuing personal growth and resilience building. They are more capable of managing stress, adjusting to change, and seeking their objectives with assurance and tenacity. Individuals with personal growth and resilience are more equipped to handle life's obstacles with courage and optimism, leading to a more contented and balanced existence.

To sum up, a happy and balanced existence requires personal development and emotional fortitude. Continuous self-improvement and self-awareness are hallmarks of personal progress, whereas emotional resilience gives one the capacity to overcome hardship and bounce back from setbacks. These ideas are mutually reinforcing, with resilience encouraging further development and personal growth enhancing resilience. A growth mindset, goal-setting, coping mechanisms, self-care, self-awareness, and creating a supportive social network are some techniques for promoting resilience and personal development. Resilience and personal development positively affect relationships with others, succeeding in the workplace, and general well-being, all of which add to a more fulfilling and meaningful existence. Prioritizing personal development and building emotional resilience can help people become more adept at navigating life's challenges, achieving their objectives, and preserving balance and fulfillment.

CHAPTER III

Effective Communication Techniques

Principles of Active Listening

A vital component of effective communication, active listening is essential for establishing rapport, understanding, and trust in interpersonal relationships. Active listening, in contrast to passive hearing, entails a conscious and focused effort to completely understand the speaker's verbal and nonverbal message. The fundamentals of active listening are examined in this section, along with its significance, essential methods, and effects on relationships and communication.

The capacity of active listening to create deep connections and clear up misconceptions makes it crucial. People who actively listen show that they appreciate and value what the other person has to say, which fosters an atmosphere that encourages candid and open communication. By actively listening, one can better understand the speaker's intentions, avoid misunderstandings, and forge stronger bonds with others. It guarantees that everyone agrees, and that problems or concerns are resolved successfully. Furthermore, active listening supports both professional and personal success by strengthening problem-solving skills, fostering collaborative efforts, and developing interpersonal skills.

Retaining complete attention is one of the core tenets of active listening. This entails minimizing distractions and providing the speaker with full attention. It's important to avoid multitasking and interrupting the speaker when you're attentively listening. Putting away electronics, maintaining eye contact, and displaying engaged body language—such as nodding and bending slightly forward—constitute full attention. By paying close attention, listeners convey that they are genuinely interested in what the speaker has to say, which fosters polite and encouraging communication.

Paraphrasing and reflecting are two more important concepts. Reflecting entails restating or summarizing what they have stated to verify understanding and demonstrate that the speaker's message has been understood correctly. Rephrasing the speaker's remarks in the listener's words is known as paraphrasing. Both strategies aid in ensuring that the audience has understood the material and offer a chance for clarification if necessary. An engaged listener can say, "It sounds like you're feeling overwhelmed by the tight deadline," in response to a speaker who expresses frustration about a project deadline. Is that accurate? This method confirms understanding and invites the speaker to go into more detail if needed.

Another essential component of active listening is empathy. To listen with compassion, one must try to comprehend the speaker's feelings and viewpoints. Even if one disagrees with the speaker's point of view, one still needs to respect and validate their feelings. Putting oneself in the speaker's position and reacting with kindness and support is the essence of empathy. When a buddy confides in you about a personal difficulty, a sympathetic listener would remark, "I understand how difficult this situation must be for you. I'm available to help you. The quality of the contact is improved when there is a sense of connection and trust created by empathetic answers.

Asking open-ended questions promotes deeper conversation and investigation and is a useful active listening strategy. Open-ended questions prompt in-depth answers and encourage the speaker to contribute details or new perspectives. These inquiries, which usually start with "how," "what," or "tell me about," help the listener gain a better comprehension of the speaker's viewpoint. An open-ended question would be, "What aspects of the presentation did you find most engaging?" instead of, "Did you like the presentation?" This method facilitates a richer exchange of ideas and meaningful conversation.

Nonverbal communication is a key component of active listening. Body language, gestures, and facial expressions are examples of non-verbal indicators important in expressing involvement and attentiveness. Nonverbal cues are another way active listeners show that they pay attention to the entire conversation and support their spoken responses. A few ways to convey interest and understanding are to keep eye contact, nod in agreement, and adopt an open posture. On the other hand, unfavorable nonverbal indicators like turning away or crossing one's arms can indicate unease or disinterest. Being aware of nonverbal cues improves the efficacy of active listening and fosters a constructive relationship.

Listening well also means controlling and putting judgment aside. It's critical to enter into talks with an open mind and refrain from assuming anything about the speaker's point of view or passing judgment too quickly. Rather than assessing or criticizing the speaker's remarks, attentive listeners concentrate on comprehending their point of view. This calls for putting aside preconceived notions and giving the present moment your whole attention. Listeners establish a secure environment for free and honest communication where the speaker feels heard and valued by putting aside their preconceived notions.

Giving feedback is just one more crucial component of active listening. Giving the speaker's message constructive and encouraging feedback is known as feedback. It may involve restating the main ideas, expressing empathy for the speaker, and making pertinent observations or recommendations. Giving the audience constructive criticism shows that you appreciate their opinions and encourages them to stay engaged. For instance, a listener may offer input following a colleague's project update by stating, "You've made great progress on this project." Although you've faced some difficulties, your strategy for overcoming them appears sensible. Feedback supports ongoing communication and aids in decision-making and problem-solving.

Being patient and letting the speaker finish expressing their ideas are other components of active listening. Patience is essential to guarantee that the speaker has enough time to deliver their point without feeling hurried or interrupted. Proactive listeners allow the speaker the time necessary to fully express their ideas and refrain from making snap judgments or answering too soon. This kind of patience promotes a more thorough comprehension of the speaker's viewpoint and a more deliberate and polite conversation.

Active listening has a wider range of effects on interpersonal and professional connections than individual exchanges. Active listening builds emotional ties, fosters understanding between partners, and improves relationship satisfaction in interpersonal interactions. It makes it possible for people to effectively handle and resolve problems, develop mutual trust, and provide genuine support to one another. Active listening is crucial for good teamwork, leadership, and client relationships in the workplace. Ensuring all stakeholders are informed and aligned promotes productivity, boosts problem-solving skills, and enables collaboration.

To sum up, active listening is an essential component of good communication that includes paying close attention, thinking back and summarizing, evoking empathy, posing open-ended questions, and using nonverbal cues. It also calls for exercising patience, giving constructive criticism, maintaining composure, and promoting polite and encouraging relationships. Active listening practices build relationships, facilitate meaningful and fruitful dialogues, and improve communication efficacy in general. People can settle problems, enhance their interpersonal skills, and foster more engaging and positive communication environments by actively listening. Active listening has numerous advantages in both the personal and professional spheres, where it is essential for promoting mutual respect, understanding, and successful teamwork.

Assertive Communication

Regarding personal and professional relationships, assertive communication is essential because it allows people to respectfully and clearly express their needs, wants, and views. It serves as a counterbalance to both passive and aggressive communication styles, guaranteeing that one's rights and ideas are expressed while also considering other people's viewpoints. The foundations of assertive communication are examined in this section, along with its advantages and useful tactics for cultivating and applying assertiveness in various settings.

Fundamentally, assertive communication is expressing oneself honestly and directly while respecting the rights and perspectives of others. It is distinguished by the straightforward and unambiguous communication of needs and wants while upholding respect for oneself and other people. Assertive communication guarantees that one's opinions are expressed honestly, unlike passive communication, which may entail avoiding conflict or neglecting to communicate genuine feelings. It also stands in contrast to aggressive communication, which can be hostile, dominating, or disrespectful. To be assertive, a person must balance advocating for their interests and paying attention to the needs and rights of others.

Increasing confidence and self-worth is one of the main advantages of assertive communication. People affirm their values and ability when they communicate politely and clearly. In addition to increasing confidence, this self-affirmation technique gives one stronger control over their interactions and relationships. People who speak assertively are likelier to accomplish their objectives, settle disputes amicably, and build deeper, more respectful relationships with others.

Additionally, assertive communication fosters healthier relationships by encouraging candid and open discussion. People are more inclined to express their intentions and sentiments directly, which lessens the likelihood of misunderstandings and misinterpretations. This clarity promotes mutual respect and trust between the parties because it shows a willingness to have productive talks rather than avoiding or confronting them. Mutual respect and understanding, which are fostered by aggressive communication, are hallmarks of healthy relationships. This method allows disagreements and helpful criticism to be voiced without inciting hate or anger.

The efficacy of assertive communication is attributed to using multiple critical methods in its practice. One crucial tactic is using "I" statements, which emphasize expressing individual sentiments and viewpoints over assigning blame or making demands. Rather than uttering, "You never listen to me," an aggressive communicator should instead remark, "I feel frustrated when I am not heard during our conversations." This method lessens defensiveness and fosters a more fruitful conversation by assisting in communicating feelings without accusing or criticizing the other person.

Keeping a cool head and a collected expression is another tactic for aggressive speaking. This entails speaking in an even tone, keeping suitable eye contact, and displaying open body language. Presenting with poise and assurance communicates confidence and sincerity, facilitating audience engagement with the message. Additionally, because the emphasis is kept on positive communication rather than emotional outbursts, it helps prevent confrontations from worsening.

Another essential component of forceful communication is setting boundaries. Boundaries serve to safeguard people's rights and well-being by defining what conduct is appropriate. People can control expectations and stop others from going too far or encroaching on their personal space by setting and sharing boundaries. For example, an aggressive answer to a colleague who constantly interrupts during meetings could be, "I would appreciate it if we could allow each person to finish their thoughts before moving on to the next speaker." Establishing and enforcing boundaries enhances an orderly and polite interaction environment.

By exhibiting a sincere interest in and comprehension of the other person's viewpoint, active listening enhances forceful communication. Giving the speaker your undivided attention, appreciating their message, and offering comments are all components of active listening. This technique promotes a more cooperative and sympathetic dialogue while supporting the speaker's feelings. For instance, when someone complains about a project, an attentive listener could say, "I recognize that you're feeling overburdened by the effort. How can we both deal with this?" By encouraging constructive discourse, active listening strengthens the ideas behind forceful communication.

Expressing worries or differences of opinion politely and constructively is a key component in assertive conflict resolution. This necessitates concentrating on the current problem rather than personal qualities or previous grievances. An aggressive communicator would state, "I feel upset when plans are changed without notice," to resolve a problem with a buddy. Can we talk about how to communicate better regarding scheduling?" This strategy focuses on finding a solution rather than intensifying the argument, encouraging a more constructive and solution-focused exchange.

Acquiring assertive communication abilities necessitates introspection and repetition. Understanding one's communication style, identifying development opportunities, and recognizing circumstances in which assertiveness may be difficult are all components of self-awareness. One can gain important insights into their assertiveness and pinpoint areas for improvement by thinking back on previous interactions and getting input from others. Confidence and skill can be developed by practicing assertiveness in various situations, such as role-playing or progressively stepping up the level of assertiveness in regular interactions.

Additionally, context and culture have an impact on aggressive communication. When engaging with others, people should be aware of the different conventions and expectations between cultures regarding communication methods. Effective cross-cultural relationships require assertive communication skills to retain clarity and respect while adhering to cultural standards. Applying assertive communication techniques can also be guided by an awareness of contextual elements like the relationship's nature or the situation's formality.

Assertive communication is crucial for career success, leadership, and productive teamwork in professional contexts. It makes communication easier and more fruitful, improves problem-solving skills, and fosters a healthy work atmosphere. An aggressive leader can, for instance, give clear instructions, constructively handle performance concerns, and promote a cooperative team environment. Establishing and maintaining professional connections, overcoming obstacles at work, and reaching professional objectives benefit from assertive communication abilities.

Assertive communication improves emotional connection and fortifies links in interpersonal interactions. It makes it possible for people to communicate honestly about their wants and requirements, foster understanding among people, and resolve disputes amicably. Assertive people can build more meaningful and healthy relationships because they are characterized by good communication, respect, and trust.

To sum up, communicating assertively is essential for promoting courteous and productive relationships in both personal and professional settings. It entails having an honest and open communication style while honoring the rights and viewpoints of others. Establishing limits, staying composed, using "I" statements, and engaging in active listening are all essential components of assertive communication. Effective dispute resolution, positive relationships, and self-esteem are all enhanced by assertive communication. Becoming an assertive person takes practice, self-awareness, and knowledge of environmental and cultural aspects. People can improve their interpersonal skills, forge better bonds with others, and handle situations with assurance and deference if they can communicate assertively.

Conflict Resolution Skills

The ability to resolve conflicts constructively is a crucial competency for people in both personal and professional settings. Understanding, cooperation, and compromise are all facilitated by a set of abilities and tactics that are essential to effective conflict resolution. This section examines the necessary conflict resolution techniques, their significance, and workable methods for resolving disputes in various settings.

Effective communication is one of the fundamental abilities in conflict resolution. Since communication allows parties to express their needs, wants, and concerns effectively, it plays a crucial role in conflict resolution. To communicate effectively, one must both express their opinions and attentively listen to the other person. To engage in active listening, one must give the speaker their whole attention, acknowledge their message, and offer feedback. Finding common ground requires that all sides feel heard and understood, which is helped by this. Effective communicators, for instance, would remark, "I understand that you have concerns about the project timeline," in response to a disagreement with a colleague. Let's talk about your particular concerns to work together to find a solution. This method lessens miscommunication and promotes a cooperative environment.

Empathy is a vital trait in conflict resolution. Acknowledging and respecting other people's feelings and viewpoints is necessary for empathy. People must comprehend the other person's thoughts, feelings, and perspectives by placing themselves in their position. People can establish rapport and trust by exhibiting empathy, which facilitates the resolution of problems. For example, when a team member becomes irate over a project delay, demonstrating empathy could mean stating, "I understand that this delay is stressful for you." Let's investigate how we might help each other through this and address your concerns. Effective conflict resolution depends on developing a supportive atmosphere where all parties are treated with respect and feel appreciated, which empathy facilitates.

Another crucial ability in conflict resolution is problem-solving. Finding solutions together and determining the root causes of the conflict are essential components of effective problem-solving. This process entails generating ideas for possible solutions, assessing their viability, and deciding on a plan of action. Solving problems necessitates being adaptable and open to different viewpoints. When two departments disagree over how to allocate resources, a problem-solving strategy might include calling a meeting to review each department's requirements, looking into potential compromises, and creating a plan that considers both sides' concerns. People can advantageously settle disputes for all parties concerned by concentrating on coming up with solutions that both parties can agree with.

Problem-solving and negotiation work hand in hand, and negotiation is an essential conflict resolution skill. Talking and negotiating are steps in coming to a mutually agreeable solution. A willingness to compromise, aggressiveness, and clarity are necessary for effective negotiating. It's critical to go into talks knowing exactly what you want from the other side and keeping an open mind about their requirements. Effective negotiation, for instance, can entail putting out counterproposals that consider both sides' concerns and working toward a mutually beneficial solution in a contract dispute. In addition to resolving the current issue, effective negotiating builds rapport by exhibiting cooperation and respect.

Another essential component of conflict resolution is emotional management. Conflicts frequently trigger strong emotions, which can affect communication and decision-making. Recognizing, controlling, and comprehending one's feelings and those of others are necessary for effective conflict resolution. Remaining composed, engaging in mindfulness exercises, and employing relaxation techniques are some methods for handling emotions. For example, if a contentious conversation starts, pausing to gather one's thoughts before answering can prevent things from getting worse and guarantee a more deliberate and productive discussion. Effective emotion management allows people to stay focused on the conflict's resolution rather than allowing their feelings to divert them.

Another key component of conflict resolution is establishing and sustaining connections. Constructive conflict resolution is facilitated by trust, respect, and good communication, which are the foundations of strong relationships. Putting money into relationship-building activities, like team-building exercises or routine check-ins, can assist in keeping tensions low and foster a constructive climate for resolving problems. For instance, planning team-building exercises to enhance connections and communication might help prevent future arguments and promote a more cooperative environment if disagreements occur within the team.

Not only may conflict resolution techniques be used to resolve immediate issues, but they can also be used to stop problems from worsening. People may foster a more harmonious and productive environment by learning and using these abilities. Resolving conflicts effectively promotes stronger bonds, better collaboration, and higher levels of pleasure. It gives people the confidence to deal with problems positively and fosters a respectful, cooperative culture.

The ability to resolve conflicts needs awareness of oneself and practice. People can gain from giving and receiving feedback, attending training sessions, and reflecting on their experiences resolving disputes. For instance, participating in role-playing games or workshops can provide participants with insightful knowledge about successful conflict-resolution strategies and boost their self-assurance while using these abilities. Moreover, getting input from mentors or coworkers can help with personal development by providing direction on areas that need work.

Conflict resolution abilities are crucial in professional settings for handling disagreements at work and creating a happy atmosphere. Effective dispute resolution can result in better team dynamics, increased productivity, and increased employee satisfaction. For example, a manager who effectively settles disputes between team members can avert interruptions, encourage cooperation, and build a stronger team. The ability to resolve conflicts in interpersonal relationships builds closer, more satisfying bonds. Constructive conflict resolution enables people to increase communication, develop trust, and fortify their bonds with friends and family.

To sum up, successful and constructive ways to resolve disagreements and disputes depend on having strong conflict resolution skills. Effective communication, empathy, problem-solving, negotiation, emotion control, and relationship-building are essential abilities. These abilities help to settle disputes, strengthen bonds, and foster a cooperative and happy atmosphere. Developing conflict resolution abilities requires experience, self-awareness, and a willingness to have productive conversations. By acquiring these competencies, people can improve their capacity to resolve disputes, forge closer bonds with others, and cultivate a more peaceful and efficient atmosphere.

Non-Verbal Communication

One essential component of human connection is non-verbal communication, which is the exchange of messages without using words. It includes a broad spectrum of actions and indicators, including posture, eye contact, tone of voice, body language, facial emotions, and gestures. Since nonverbal communication frequently provides more information than verbal communication alone, it is essential to comprehend and interpret it for successful interpersonal relationships. The importance of nonverbal communication, its several forms, and its effects on interpersonal and professional relationships are all examined in this section.

Facial expressions are one of the main elements of nonverbal communication. Many different emotions, including happiness, sadness, anger, surprise, and disgust, can be expressed through the human face. These idioms are frequently culturally ubiquitous and recognizable. For example, a grin usually conveys warmth and appreciation, whereas a frown could express concern or annoyance. In interactions, facial expressions give instant feedback, enabling people to assess the emotional condition of others and reply accordingly quickly. They are also essential for building connections and evoking empathy. For instance, a teacher who smiles at a student is likely to foster a more friendly and encouraging learning atmosphere. Still, one who displays sternness may prevent students from communicating freely.

Another crucial component of nonverbal communication is body language. It consists of posture, motions, and gestures that imply meaning without using words. Intentional motions like thumbs-ups and handshakes can be considered gestures, as can unintentional ones like fidgeting or crossing arms. A person's confidence, openness, or defensiveness can be inferred from their body language. For example, receptiveness and engagement are typically indicated by open and relaxed body language, such as uncrossed arms and a small forward lean. On the other hand, defensive or closed body language, like bending over and crossing arms, can convey unease or reluctance. By interpreting the underlying emotions and attitudes of others through body language, people may communicate and engage with others more effectively.

Body language and posture are strongly related. Posture refers to how people stand or sit. One's involvement, confidence, and authority level can be inferred from their posture. For instance, slouching or shrinking back may convey nervousness or indifference, whereas standing straight with shoulders back and head held high might convey confidence and assertiveness. In work environments, one's posture can affect how competent and leadership-like someone is perceived. While a slouched posture could be detrimental to a leader's authority, an open, erect posture will likely inspire confidence and compel respect. In addition to influencing, one's perception and response from others, posture plays a crucial role in interpersonal relationships.

Making eye contact is essential to establishing rapport and trust in nonverbal communication. Sustaining suitable eye contact conveys focus, genuineness, and involvement in a dialogue. It facilitates the development of understanding and a sense of connectedness. On the other hand, not making eye contact may be interpreted as indifference, evasiveness, or discomfort. However, different cultures have different standards for eye contact, some value direct eye contact more than others. For example, extended eye contact may be regarded as disrespectful in some Asian cultures. In contrast, persistent eye contact is often recognized as a sign of confidence and honesty in Western societies. Preventing miscommunication and improving cross-cultural communication can be achieved by being aware of cultural variations in eye contact.

Pitch, loudness, pace, and inflection of spoken language are all included in a tone of voice, also known as paralanguage. It can express attitudes and feelings that the words do not specifically articulate. In contrast, a harsh or monotonous tone may indicate irritation or apathy. For instance, a warm and energetic tone might represent friendship and encouragement. Speaking with a tone of voice gives spoken communication more depth by adding more emotional nuance and context. The tone of voice can affect how messages are understood and received professionally. A manager who gives feedback in an upbeat and motivational manner is more likely to create a happy and productive work atmosphere. On the other hand, a critical or dismissive tone can lower productivity and employee morale.

Proxemics, the term for using personal space and physical distance in interactions, is another aspect of nonverbal communication. Cultural conventions about personal space differ, affecting people's comfort levels during social encounters. For example, while certain cultures encourage intimacy during interactions, others can favor greater personal space. Effective cross-cultural communication requires an awareness of and respect for these cultural variances in proxemics. Personal space can foster a courteous and upbeat work atmosphere in professional environments when used appropriately. While keeping the proper distance can promote pleasant and productive encounters, crossing personal boundaries can be interpreted as rude or intrusive.

Verbal communication is frequently enhanced and complemented by nonverbal communication. It adds more context, supports spoken words, and clarifies meaning. The message is reinforced when a manager gives an employee verbal praise and demonstrates real gratitude with good body language, like smiling and nodding. Nonverbal cues are another useful tool for improving communication, particularly in miscommunication or language limitations. For example, when words alone are insufficient, adding gestures or facial expressions can help convey meaning. People can improve communication effectiveness and increase clarity by matching nonverbal clues with spoken words.

Conflicts and misunderstandings can result from misinterpreting nonverbal cues. People may interpret non-verbal cues differently depending on their cultural background and personal experiences because they can be subtle and context-dependent. For example, a gesture regarded as kind in one culture could be seen as disrespectful in another. It's critical to consider the context of non-verbal cues and ask questions when necessary to reduce misinterpretations. Resolving any misunderstandings and ensuring efficient communication is possible by having an honest and polite conversation.

Gaining insight into nonverbal communication helps strengthen bonds and advance interpersonal abilities. People can learn more about the dynamics of their interactions and make necessary modifications by being aware of their non-verbal signs and those of others. For instance, improving one's awareness of one's voice and body language can lead to better connections and more successful communication. Comparably, interpreting nonverbal cues from others can reveal important details about their emotions and behaviors, facilitating more sensitive and understanding dialogue.

Nonverbal communication abilities are critical for efficient teamwork, customer relations, and leadership in work environments. Leaders skilled at communicating confidence, support, and empathy through nonverbal cues have a higher chance of inspiring and motivating their staff. Team members can work together more productively and resolve possible problems before they get out of hand if they know each other's nonverbal cues. Recognizing and addressing nonverbal signs in customer service can improve client satisfaction and foster strong connections. For example, a customer care agent can deliver a more successful and personalized experience if they can read and react to the customer's body language and tone.

Nonverbal communication is essential in interpersonal interactions for expressing feelings, developing closeness, and settling disputes. Observing one another's nonverbal signs allows couples to improve their emotional bond and deal with problems more skillfully. For instance, it can be easier to have supportive and empathic interactions when one partner's nonverbal cues of discomfort or suffering are recognized and addressed. Body language, eye contact, and physical touch are examples of non-verbal communication that helps convey love and gratitude.

In summary, nonverbal cues, including posture, tone of voice, eye contact, facial emotions, and body language, play a significant role in human interaction. It is important for establishing rapport, expressing feelings, and improving spoken communication. Gaining an understanding of and ability to read nonverbal signs can enhance communication, avoid misunderstandings, and promote healthy relationships. Understanding nonverbal communication and using it skillfully can improve relationships in both personal and professional settings, resulting in more fulfilling and fruitful communication experiences. Understanding the subtleties of nonverbal communication helps people connect more successfully and harmoniously by facilitating more effortless navigation of social dynamics.

Constructive Feedback

Giving and receiving constructive feedback helps people grow personally and professionally by giving them the knowledge and direction they need to enhance their abilities, behaviors, and performance. Contrary to critical or negative feedback, which could highlight flaws, constructive criticism aims to promote development and progress by being helpful and encouraging. This section examines the fundamentals of constructive criticism, its significance, and useful methods for giving and receiving feedback productively.

Constructive criticism is fundamentally defined by its emphasis on particular, doable recommendations for improvement. It targets areas where people can improve their performance or change their behavior to support intended results or objectives. Clear, unbiased, and based on observed behaviors rather than personal qualities, constructive criticism is effective. Constructive feedback, for instance, would highlight particular behaviors rather than generalizations such as, "You're not a good team player." An example of this might be, "During the last project, there were instances where you missed team meetings and deadlines." It would help if you got better at communicating with the team and attending events. This method aids people in understanding precisely which behaviors should be altered and why.

A culture of learning and continual growth requires constructive criticism. Employees can grow their talents and perform professionally when they know their strengths and flaws. When a manager gives a worker constructive criticism, for instance, they could point out the worker's strong points—like problem-solving—and offer concrete solutions for their areas of improvement, like time management. This well-rounded strategy increases motivation and self-assurance in addition to fostering skill development. Constructive feedback increases an employee's sense of engagement and value, which boosts productivity and job happiness.

Timeliness is one of the most important aspects of constructive criticism. Feedback should be given as soon as feasible after the behavior or event to ensure that feedback is applicable and useful. Feedback given too late may lose its significance and impact, making it more difficult for recipients to relate the comments to their behavior. Giving comments on a presentation right away, for example, enables the speaker to remember particular elements of their performance and incorporate the recommendations into future talks. Individuals can make changes in real time when they receive timely feedback, which promotes more rapid improvements and improved learning outcomes.

The notion of specificity is also crucial. Detailed comments targeted at particular habits or results are preferable to general or ambiguous remarks when providing constructive criticism. People who receive specific comments can better pinpoint exactly what needs to change and why. A more targeted feedback statement may be, "The section on data analysis in your report was difficult to follow because it lacked clear explanations of the statistical methods used," as opposed to, "Your report was unclear." Clarity would be improved by including a synopsis of these techniques and their ramifications. Individuals can use specific comments to gain actionable insights and create focused adjustments.

Additionally, it is important to provide constructive criticism politely and encouragingly. Feedback's delivery and tone can greatly impact how it's taken in and understood. Constructive criticism is when comments are given in an upbeat and supportive way, emphasizing progress over condemnation. For instance, a constructive feedback strategy can use words like, "I noticed that you faced challenges with the project deadline," rather than a harsh tone or accusatory language. Let's talk about a few techniques that can make time management easier for you in the future. This encouraging method promotes a more cooperative and upbeat atmosphere by making people feel more at ease and open to criticism.

It's critical to weigh feedback's good and negative parts while providing constructive criticism. This method, sometimes known as the "sandwich" strategy, consists of giving encouraging comments first, emphasizing areas that want work, and ending with more encouraging words. For instance, a manager might start by praising a worker for their excellent work on a recent project, then offer detailed recommendations for how the worker might improve in various areas and conclude by showcasing the worker's potential and overall accomplishments. This well-rounded strategy encourages people to see feedback as a chance for personal development rather than as a means of criticizing them, which helps people stay motivated.

Effectively receiving constructive criticism is also essential for both professional and personal growth. People with a growth mentality and receptive to criticism are more likely to gain from the advice. This entails listening intently to criticism, seeking clarification, and considering the recommendations made. An individual can, for example, ask for instances of particular circumstances where communication could be improved and look for extra resources or training to build these skills if feedback includes a suggestion to improve communication skills. People who accept criticism as a teaching tool rather than a personal jab are more likely to stay motivated and dedicated to their growth.

People must act proactively to put the advice given into practice and be receptive to criticism. This includes establishing objectives, formulating plans of action, and tracking developments. An individual might, for instance, create explicit goals to use time management tools, prioritize work more effectively, and monitor their progress over time after obtaining input on how to improve time management. Individuals can exhibit their dedication to personal development by diligently addressing the feedback and implementing the required modifications.

Additionally essential to team relations and teamwork is constructive feedback. Positive feedback exchanged between team members promotes a climate of respect for one another and ongoing development. This cooperative method facilitates problem-solving, improves output, and forges closer professional bonds. A team that participates in constructive feedback sessions regularly is likely to see an improvement in trust, better communication, and overall performance. Teams can better overcome obstacles and accomplish their objectives by accepting feedback as a regular practice.

Constructive criticism is frequently employed in professional development programs as a coaching and mentoring technique. Mentors and coaches offer direction and encouragement to help people grow as people, accomplish their objectives, and get beyond challenges. This process requires constructive criticism since it sheds light on both areas of strength and need for development. A mentor could offer input on a person's leadership style, make recommendations for improving their efficacy, and provide tools for continued growth. Individuals are assisted in realizing their full potential and are supported in their personal improvement journey by this customized feedback.

To sum up, constructive criticism is essential to both professional and personal growth since it gives people the understanding and direction they need to enhance their abilities and performance. People can promote development by concentrating on precise, doable recommendations, providing feedback in a timely and encouraging way, and weighing the positive and bad elements. To maximize constructive criticism, one must embrace feedback as a learning opportunity, receive it with an open mind, and move proactively to put suggestions into practice. Constructive criticism fosters better bonds, increased performance, and a continual development culture in both personal and professional settings.

CHAPTER IV

Transforming Toxic Interactions

Identifying Toxic Behaviors

Maintaining positive connections in both personal and professional spheres requires recognizing harmful behaviors. Behaviors that weaken, harm, or interfere with relationships are considered toxic and frequently create an unfavorable atmosphere. Acknowledging these actions is the first step in dealing with them and lessening their effects. This section examines the traits of toxic behaviors, how they affect people and relationships, and practical methods for recognizing and controlling them.

Although toxic behaviors can take many different forms, they are frequently typified by negative, hostile, and manipulative tendencies. Manipulation is a prevalent harmful behavior in which people attempt to control or influence others by force or dishonesty. This can involve emotional blackmail, gaslighting, or guilt-tripping. For example, a coworker may be manipulated if they constantly diminish another's efforts by blaming their achievements on chance rather than talent. Manipulation undermines confidence and fosters a climate where people feel powerless and undercut.

Another common type of toxic behavior is antagonism, including criticism, hatred, and aggression directed against others. Hostile people frequently show anger through sarcasm, harsh language, or passive-aggressive behavior. For example, a boss who often minimizes staff members during meetings or uses derogatory language to criticize their job can create a toxic work environment. Effectively managing and addressing hostile behaviors is crucial since they can result in strained relationships, low morale, and lower productivity.

Another important characteristic of harmful conduct is negativity. People constantly fixated on issues rather than finding solutions, moaning, or propagating negativity can all contribute to a poisonous environment. A negative culture might be established, for example, by an employee who consistently criticizes organizational changes without providing helpful criticism or other suggestions. This widespread negativity has the potential to lower motivation, impede teamwork, and foster an atmosphere where people are demoralized and disengaged.

A crucial attribute of toxic conduct is the absence of responsibility. People with poisonous attitudes frequently deny their part in disputes or unfavorable circumstances. They could place the blame elsewhere, confess their wrongdoings, or justify their conduct. For instance, a lack of accountability is seen in someone who regularly disrupts colleagues during meetings and then brushes off criticism about their actions as unjustified or irrelevant. This avoidance of accountability makes disputes worse and keeps them from being resolved.

Toxic actions can significantly impact relationships and individuals. Individuals who are subjected to poisonous behavior may suffer from stress, worry, and low self-esteem. For instance, workers who receive persistent criticism from management could grow to feel inadequate and lose faith in their skills. Toxic behaviors have a detrimental emotional impact that can cause burnout, disengagement, and general dissatisfaction with relationships at work or in personal life.

Toxic behaviors can negatively impact team relationships and organizational effectiveness in professional contexts. Teams with toxic members may need help to collaborate, have many disagreements, and build trust. For example, a team with dishonest and competitive members may need help to work together and communicate, which will affect output and performance. Restoring a healthy work atmosphere and ensuring that teams can operate well depend on addressing toxic behaviors.

Toxic behaviors can be recognized by looking for patterns and evaluating how they affect people and relationships. One strategy is to observe any disagreements or recurrent problems during encounters. For instance, toxic behaviors may occur if a specific person routinely causes conflict or animosity during team meetings. Analyze with caution any patterns of negativity or manipulation that show up in talks or encounters regularly.

It's crucial to consider the environment in which hazardous behaviors occur. Stressful, competitive, or unsupportive situations may be more conducive to toxic behaviors. For instance, a high-stress workplace where staff members feel under continual observation may encourage harmful behaviors like gossip or sabotage—recognizing the larger picture aids in determining the root causes of toxic behavior and resolving systemic problems that fuel it.

It takes effective communication to recognize and deal with toxic behaviors. It might be helpful to clarify problems, voice concerns, and look for solutions by having an honest and open conversation. Toxic conduct, for instance, can be addressed head-on with the offending party courteously and productively to determine the underlying causes and move toward remedies. Instead of laying blame or intensifying arguments, it's critical to approach these discussions with empathy and a focus on establishing common ground.

To resolve harmful behaviors, seeking outside support could occasionally be essential. This may entail consulting a counselor, mediator, or HR specialist who can offer dispassionate viewpoints and assist in settling. A mediator could be useful in a company where toxic habits are deeply ingrained, as they can resolve issues and create plans for enhancing team chemistry. Effective management and resolution of poisonous behaviors can be facilitated by the additional resources and skills that external support can offer.

Establishing a welcoming and encouraging environment that promotes constructive relationships and proactively handles problems is essential to controlling and preventing toxic behaviors. Toxic behaviors can be reduced by establishing explicit rules and regulations for conduct, encouraging honest communication, and cultivating an environment that values responsibility and respect. A more upbeat and cooperative atmosphere can be created, for instance, by clearly outlining standards for behavior and offering training in effective communication and dispute resolution.

Finding and correcting toxic behaviors can also be aided by routine performance reviews and feedback. Both individuals and organizations can address problems before they become more serious and encourage positive behavior by giving constructive criticism and establishing clear performance goals. Toxic behaviors can be avoided, and people can be made aware of the significance of preserving a healthy work environment by having a manager who, for instance, sets clear standards for behavior and gives frequent feedback.

It is crucial to understand that dealing with toxic behaviors is a continuous process that calls for dedication and work from all parties. Creating a happy and healthy atmosphere requires ongoing observation, evaluation, and modification. For instance, a positive and productive environment can be maintained by routinely evaluating team dynamics, offering input opportunities, and resolving problems as they arise.

To sum up, recognizing toxic behaviors is critical to preserving wholesome interpersonal and professional connections. Negativity, aggression, manipulation, and a lack of accountability are traits of harmful behaviors that can have a serious negative impact on people and relationships. It takes an examination of patterns, an evaluation of effects, and contextual considerations to identify these behaviors. The three most important tactics for dealing with and controlling toxic behaviors are good communication, getting outside help, and fostering a positive atmosphere. People and organizations can improve relationships, encourage healthy interactions, and increase overall performance by proactively addressing toxic behaviors and creating a supportive environment.

Addressing Toxicity in Yourself

Toxic self-reaction is a necessary first step toward healing relationships and personal development. Negativity, manipulation, aggression, and a lack of accountability are harmful behaviors that can significantly negatively influence one's social interactions and overall well-being. Being honest, self-aware, and dedicated to changing oneself are necessary for identifying and dealing with these habits. This section examines how to recognize toxic qualities in oneself, comprehend the causes of those traits, and take proactive measures to promote relationships and personal development.

Identifying and resolving these habits is the first step toward dealing with toxicity. Self-reflection, in which people consider their deeds, recurring patterns of conduct, and effects on others, is frequently the first step in this process. For instance, when faced with difficulties, one may constantly observe a propensity to criticize or place the blame elsewhere. This awareness is important because it enables people to face their actions instead of ignoring them or putting the blame elsewhere. Techniques like writing, meditation, or asking reliable friends or coworkers for feedback can all help with self-reflection. Honest self-evaluation enables people to see behavioral patterns causing a toxic work environment.

Effectively resolving toxic habits requires an understanding of their underlying origins. One of the main causes of toxicity is frequently an unmet need, an unresolved emotional conflict, or a traumatic history. For instance, someone who uses manipulation often may do it to impose power over others or make up for feelings of inferiority. Examining these root reasons necessitates reflection and, usually, expert assistance. To explore the deeper psychological and emotional causes of toxic behaviors, therapy or counseling can be quite helpful. Through addressing these underlying causes, people can start to resolve their problems and lessen the possibility that harmful behavior will resurface.

The next stage is to create change management methods after recognizing harmful behaviors and their causes. This entails formulating an action plan for particular behaviors and establishing precise improvement goals. For example, if they realize they do so often, someone may practice straightforward and honest communication instead of passive-aggressive communication. Making an action plan could entail undertaking tasks like picking up new communication skills, getting input from others, and routinely assessing results. Since changing ingrained behavioral habits can be difficult, putting these changes into practice will take dedication and consistency.

The ability to recognize oneself is essential to this process. Awareness of one's actions and responses enables people to identify hazardous behaviors before they become more severe. One can deliberately decide to change their attention to constructive or positive alternatives, for instance, if they notice falling into a negative cycle under stressful conditions. Self-awareness is being aware of one's thoughts, feelings, and triggers to make deliberate decisions about one's actions. Self-monitoring and mindfulness are two strategies that can assist people in being aware of their actions and modifying them as necessary.

Developing emotional intelligence is yet another essential part of dealing with poison. Emotional intelligence is the capacity to identify, comprehend, and regulate one's emotions and those of others. People can lessen the possibility of toxic interactions and enhance their interpersonal abilities by increasing emotional intelligence. This entails developing constructive conflict resolution skills, stress management techniques, and understanding and empathic communication skills. For instance, deep breathing, relaxation techniques, or cognitive restructuring may help someone with trouble controlling their anger better manage their emotions.

Self-compassion and forgiveness are also crucial components in dealing with poison. When someone recognizes harmful behaviors in themselves, they may experience irritation, remorse, or humiliation. Treating oneself with kindness and understanding instead of self-criticism is key to practicing self-compassion. Healing and the release of negative emotions can be facilitated by forgiveness—both toward oneself and toward others. For instance, accepting that everyone makes mistakes and engaging in forgiveness practices might support someone feeling guilty about past deeds and enable them to move on and concentrate on making positive changes.

Effective communication is one of the most important skills for controlling and minimizing harmful behaviors. Improving one's capacity for polite, forceful, and clear communication can help avoid miscommunications and confrontations. For instance, a person who exhibits passive-aggressive behavior may want to practice making direct and positive use of "I" words to communicate their emotions. For example, rather than implying something about the actions of a coworker, they may state something like, "It annoys me when meetings start late because it interferes with my schedule." Can we cooperate to make sure we get started on time? Toxic behaviors are less likely to occur when clear and courteous communication promotes healthy interactions.

Getting input from other people can also be helpful when dealing with toxicity. Speaking candidly and openly with mentors, coworkers, or trusted friends can give important insights into one's behavior and its effects. People can track their progress and identify areas for development using constructive criticism. For instance, someone trying to lessen their propensity to interrupt others can inquire about their progress and whether they are becoming more effective communicators. This input can strengthen the resolve to make changes and provide fresh viewpoints.

Establishing limits is another crucial tactic for controlling harmful conduct and setting up explicit boundaries aids people in safeguarding their personal health and sustaining civil relationships with others. For example, if someone discovers that they are frequently overpowered by the demands or bad behavior of others, establishing boundaries may entail stating their availability limits or firmly confronting unacceptable behavior. It is important to set and convey boundaries respectfully and respectfully for oneself and others.

It's crucial to develop constructive habits and behaviors that promote personal development and wholesome relationships and deal with poisonous tendencies one may exhibit. This involves doing things that make you happy, like working out, taking up a hobby, and hanging out with positive people. For instance, combining regular exercise with relaxation methods can reduce stress and enhance emotional toughness. Developing healthy habits lowers the chance of reverting to unhealthy behaviors and promotes a more balanced and satisfying existence.

Sustaining change and keeping up progress calls for constant work and introspection. Assessing behavior, reviewing objectives, and making corrections routinely is critical. For instance, someone who has improved their communication style can evaluate how they address disagreements regularly and determine whether any changes need to be made. Positive improvements are sustained and reinforced over time with the support of ongoing self-reflection and a dedication to personal development.

Taking care of one's toxicity is a life-changing process that calls for self-awareness, understanding the underlying causes, and applying practical change management techniques. Toxic habits can be identified, their causes investigated, and skills like emotional intelligence, effective communication, and self-compassion developed. These actions allow people to grow personally and enhance relationships. Creating boundaries, asking for feedback, and establishing positive habits to maintain change and encourage a more satisfying life are also critical. People can overcome toxic tendencies and cultivate more positive, courteous, and supportive relationships with others if they put in the necessary effort and commitment.

Handling Toxicity in Others

Managing others' toxicity is essential for preserving well-being and developing wholesome connections. Whether in social encounters, professional settings, or personal relationships, toxic behaviors can have a profound effect on people and their surroundings. To effectively confront and manage toxicity, one must be aware of these behaviors, establish boundaries, use constructive interaction techniques, and know when to get outside help. This section explores the process of handling toxic people, offering solutions and tactics for handling these difficult circumstances.

Recognizing the symptoms and patterns of toxic behavior in others is the first step in managing their toxicity. A variety of actions, such as manipulation, hatred, negativity, and a lack of accountability, can be indicators of toxic behaviors. Toxic qualities include, for example, persistently undermining others' efforts or communicating in a passive-aggressive manner. It takes careful observation and knowledge of how these behaviors impact relationships and interactions to identify these behaviors. People ought to be aware of persistent problems or disputes and how other people's actions affect their welfare and the environment in general. Understanding these patterns is essential to creating tactics that effectively control and deal with toxic conduct.

Establishing healthy and transparent boundaries is crucial after harmful behavior has been recognized. Boundaries operate as limits to preserve one's emotional and psychological health and ensure polite relationships. Setting a boundary could entail, for instance, confronting a coworker who often interrupts or minimizes one's contributions in meetings aggressively and directly. "I need to finish my point before we move on," someone could say. Please allow me to finish my thinking. Setting limits calls for regularity and unambiguous communication. Establishing courteous yet strong boundaries ensures they are recognized and adhered to. Establishing limits keeps interactions civil and balanced while halting the progression of poisonous behavior.

Managing others' toxicity requires effective communication. Having polite, direct conversations can help avoid misconceptions and handle problems head-on. Utilizing "I" phrases to voice sentiments and concerns without assigning blame when addressing harmful behavior is critical. For example, you may say, "I feel uncomfortable when you speak to me in that tone," instead of calling someone unpleasant. Can we have a more relaxed conversation about this? Instead of making accusations that can provoke defensiveness and more confrontation, this method focuses on communicating personal experiences and sentiments. Positive transformation is encouraged, and a productive environment is fostered by courteous and clear communication.

It's critical to control one's reactions and emotions when interacting with toxic people. Strong emotional emotions like annoyance, rage, or anxiety can be triggered by toxic behavior. Self-regulation practices like mindfulness, deep breathing, and cognitive reframing can support people in staying calm and responding intelligently. For instance, rather than reacting rashly to someone always criticizing, one could pause, evaluate the circumstances, control their feelings, and determine the best course of action. Controlling one's emotions keeps encounters from spiraling out of control and turning into a battlefield for unresolved issues.

Conflict resolution strategies could be essential in certain situations to handle toxic conduct properly. Conflict resolution involves finding common ground, addressing the underlying problems, and devising a workable solution. For example, having a systematic conversation to investigate the underlying issues and jointly devise solutions might help overcome recurrent conflicts with friends or coworkers. Methods like problem-solving, in which both parties collaborate to discover a solution, and active listening, in which one listens intently and sympathetically to the other party's perspective, can be successful. Conflict resolution aims to address the root causes of toxicity and foster a more constructive and cooperative atmosphere.

Determining if the poisonous conduct is a pattern that may be addressed by discussion and resolution or if it is a more persistent problem is also essential. It could be necessary to reevaluate the dynamics of the relationship or interactions if toxic conduct continues despite efforts to remedy it. For instance, putting strong boundaries on interactions or severing ties with someone could be justified if their behavior is persistently destructive and unyielding. Carefully weighing the effects on one's well-being and the likelihood of preserving a good relationship can help you make this decision. When toxicity is unmanageable, putting one's own mental and emotional well-being first may mean cutting off or removing contact with the toxic person.

Getting outside help can be helpful when handling toxic conduct that is severe or chronic. This support can take many forms, such as working with human resources in a company context, engaging in professional therapy, or mediating disputes. Counselors and therapists with professional training can offer direction and techniques for handling challenging situations and resolving underlying problems. Mediation services can help foster productive discussion and dispute resolution when direct communication has failed. In the workplace context, human resources can assist in methodically addressing toxic conduct and guaranteeing the necessary steps to provide a healthy work environment.

Toxic behavior can also be lessened by creating a supportive and upbeat atmosphere in addition to these tactics. Toxic contacts can be mitigated, and better interactions can be fostered by fostering an environment of respect, candid communication, and mutual support. For example, promoting cooperation, praising contributions, and supporting teammates can foster a more pleasant dynamic in a team environment. People can lessen the effects of toxic conduct and contribute to a more enjoyable and peaceful workplace by encouraging positive behaviors and creating a supportive environment.

Managing toxicity in others requires self-management, boundary-setting, effective communication, and awareness. Toxic behaviors must be identified, boundaries must be established, and constructive communication methods must be used to manage relationships and settle disputes. Using conflict resolution strategies, controlling one's reactions, and, when needed, obtaining outside assistance are other strategies for effectively managing toxic conduct. People can manage toxic relationships and preserve healthier, more positive ones by putting their well-being first and creating a supportive environment.

Resilience, sensitivity, and patience are necessary for the difficult and continuous process of dealing with other people's toxicity. People can effectively handle toxic behaviors and promote more respectful and good interactions by sticking to these tactics and focusing on constructive alternatives. It is possible to manage and overcome the difficulties presented by toxic conduct, ultimately leading to healthier and more rewarding relationships with careful effort and mindful interaction.

Turning Negative Interactions into Positive Outcomes

The ability to transform unfavorable interactions into advantageous ones is essential for promoting personal development, strengthening bonds with others, and elevating general well-being. Negative interactions can profoundly affect people and their relationships, regardless of the source—conflicts, miscommunications, or poisonous behaviors. However, if handled correctly, these difficult circumstances can become chances for development, education, and better relationships. This section examines methods for transforming unfavorable encounters into advantageous results, emphasizing good communication, empathy, constructive problem-solving, and introspection.

Effective communication is the first step in changing unfavorable interactions. Communicating effectively takes straightforward expression of oneself, attentive listening, and direct issue resolution. It is imperative to adopt an attitude of openness and inquiry instead of defensiveness when confronted with a negative interaction. De-escalating a situation can be achieved, for example, by gently addressing a disagreement during a meeting and attempting to comprehend the other person's viewpoint. A potentially unfavorable interaction can be transformed into a productive conversation by prioritizing mutual understanding in a dialogue rather than reacting hastily or concentrating just on one's complaints. Effective communication requires active listening, which is giving the speaker your whole attention, acknowledging their ideas, and intelligently answering. One way to help people discover common ground and resolve problems amicably is to promote a courteous and open exchange of views.

When it comes to turning unpleasant contacts into positive ones, empathy is essential. Navigating disagreements and misunderstandings requires empathy, which is the capacity to comprehend and experience another person's feelings. Reacting empathetically to negative behavior, such as criticism or hate, can assist in diffusing the situation and promote a more constructive exchange. When a coworker complains about a project, demonstrating empathy by accepting their sentiments and providing support might assist in changing the focus of the conversation from assigning blame to teamwork. Empathy enables people to relate to each other more deeply, identify the underlying emotions behind the bad conduct, and healthily deal with these feelings. People can establish rapport and foster a more cooperative and supportive environment by displaying empathy and understanding.

Another essential tactic for transforming unfavorable contacts into advantageous ones is constructive problem-solving. Finding the underlying reasons for disputes, creating creative solutions, and cooperating to implement these solutions are all parts of constructive problem-solving. It's crucial to approach a negative interaction with a problem-solving mindset rather than just concentrating on the disagreement. When two team members disagree about the course of a project, for example, addressing the issue by figuring out the underlying problems and working together to create a solution can help find a workable answer. It takes imagination, open discussion, and a willingness to make concessions to solve problems constructively. People can turn disagreements into chances for development and progress by concentrating on finding answers rather than lingering on the unpleasant parts of the exchange.

Converting negative encounters into positive ones also requires introspection on one's part. Getting important insights and possibilities for self-improvement is possible by considering one's actions, responses, and contributions to the contact. For instance, if a buddy engagement ends badly, thinking back on one's behavior and analyzing how it contributed to the unfavorable result may assist in pinpointing areas that need improvement. Examining one's ideas, feelings, and behaviors through personal reflection allows one to apply this understanding to modify behavior constructively. People might approach future conversations with more awareness and efficacy if they accept responsibility for their own mistakes and mistakes in the interaction. Learning from bad experiences and applying these lessons to enhance future encounters is another personal reflection aspect. People can improve their relationships and strengthen their interpersonal skills by adopting a growth mindset and seeing unfavorable interactions as teaching opportunities.

Developing resilience is another crucial component in transforming unfavorable encounters into advantageous results. Resilience is the capacity to overcome adversity and keep a positive attitude in facing difficulties. Building a mindset that views setbacks as chances for improvement and education is essential to becoming resilient. Resilient people can remain calm under pressure, concentrate on finding answers, and resist giving up on their goals in the face of obstacles. For instance, instead of viewing a project proposal rejection as a failure, a resilient person would see it as a chance to get feedback, make changes, and try again. Positivity, emotional control, and self-awareness are necessary for developing resilience. Building resilience helps people deal with difficult situations with more assurance and flexibility.

Creating a happy atmosphere also helps to transform unfavorable contacts into advantageous ones. Promoting positive behaviors, acknowledging accomplishments, and fostering open communication are all important components of creating a supportive and productive atmosphere. For example, recognizing team members' efforts, offering helpful criticism, and promoting cooperation are ways to create a happy work atmosphere.

Negative interactions are less likely to occur in an environment that values and supports each individual, and when they do, they can be handled more skillfully. Positive encounters can be lessened, and positive results can be promoted with mutual respect, teamwork, and a focus on common objectives.

In some circumstances, seeking outside assistance could be required to address and resolve unfavorable encounters properly. There are other ways that external help can be provided, such as through professional development, counseling, or mediation. Through discussion, an impartial third party helps disputing parties come to a resolution. This process is known as mediation. Through counseling, people can learn techniques and tools for handling conflict and enhancing communication. Opportunities for professional development, such as training courses or workshops, can improve a person's interpersonal abilities and teach them strategies for managing challenging situations. Seeking outside assistance can provide fresh viewpoints, materials, and experience that can help transform unpleasant encounters into productive ones.

When handling unpleasant encounters, keeping a long-term perspective is critical. As vital as it is to resolve disputes and conflicts right away, relationships and personal development are also affected by interactions over the long term. People might approach unpleasant encounters from a wider angle by concentrating on long-term objectives including strengthening connections, developing communication skills, and creating a positive atmosphere. This long-term strategy entails realizing that unfavorable interactions frequently occur as a byproduct of a bigger process of development and growth. People focused on long-term goals can bounce back from adverse experiences and remain optimistic.

Ultimately, changing unfavorable contacts into favorable ones requires strong interpersonal skills, empathy, constructive problem-solving, introspection, resilience, and a supportive atmosphere. Conflicts can be turned into learning opportunities by having courteous, open communication, acting with empathy, and putting your attention on finding solutions. Ongoing self-improvement and adaptability are facilitated by introspection and resilience while creating a supportive environment and looking for outside assistance to offer more resources and viewpoints. People can develop stronger, more positive connections and effectively handle bad situations by implementing these tactics and keeping a long-term perspective.

Negative interaction management and transformation is a difficult and continuous process that calls for perseverance, competence, and dedication. People can use techniques for positive change and a constructive mindset to approach unfavorable encounters, which can help them transform difficult circumstances into chances for personal development. Developing healthier relationships, improving individual well-being, and creating a more positive and supportive environment is possible by working hard and keeping an eye on the end goal.

Learning from Difficult Situations

Learning from challenging circumstances is one of the most important aspects of human development and growth. Adversities and challenges test our resiliency and flexibility and teach us important lessons that improve our knowledge, abilities, and general well-being. To move forward and thrive in the face of adversity, one must be able to draw lessons from events such as personal setbacks, professional barriers, or complex social relationships. This section examines the best ways to grow from challenging circumstances by adopting a growth mindset, thinking back on events, getting feedback, and using newfound understanding to tackle problems in the future.

A growth attitude is the first step to learning from challenging circumstances. The idea that skills and intelligence can be developed via work, education, and perseverance is known as a growth mindset. People with a growth mentality see a difficult circumstance as a chance for personal development rather than a setback. A person with a growth mindset might concentrate on the lessons learned from a project's failure and think about how to go forward better if it falls short of its goals at work. This viewpoint promotes taking a proactive approach to problems, viewing setbacks as opportunities for growth rather than impassable roadblocks. Adopting a growth mindset promotes a never-ending learning and development process by keeping people resilient and motivated.

Another essential element of learning from challenging circumstances is reflection. People can assess what happened, why, and how it can be addressed by reflecting on their experiences. Examining oneself critically throughout a difficult situation entails considering one's choices, actions, and responses. If a dispute emerges within a team, it can be beneficial to consider the communication patterns, individual input, and the resolution method. Through reflective practice, people can better understand their strengths and shortcomings, see patterns in their behavior, and pinpoint areas where they need to grow. People can better understand their experiences and apply the lessons they've learned to comparable circumstances in the future by pausing to reflect on them.

Getting criticism is yet another crucial tactic for growing from challenging circumstances. Feedback offers an outside viewpoint on one's conduct, performance, and problem-solving style. Asking friends, mentors, or coworkers for criticism can help people understand how others view their choices and actions. For instance, getting input from peers or superiors following a poor presentation might highlight areas needing work, such as engagement tactics, content structure, or presentation techniques. Giving constructive criticism enables people to recognize their areas of strength and improvement, allowing them to make well-informed adjustments and improvements. Positively accepting criticism and being open to new ideas can greatly advance one's career and personal growth.

Gaining and improving from challenging experiences requires applying learned lessons to new and difficult circumstances. Upon identification of lessons and receipt of feedback, it is imperative to incorporate these insights into future scenarios. For example, if a particular method of problem-solving has yet to work in the past, using different approaches or adjusting the technique in response to criticism can improve results in the future. This process is part of setting objectives, creating action plans, and regularly assessing results. By applying insights and required modifications, people can enhance their ability to handle similar challenges by building on previous experiences. By taking the initiative, you can make sure that the lessons you acquire during trying times are put to good use and promote development instead of being thrown away.

Resilience is essential for learning from challenging circumstances. The capacity to overcome obstacles, adjust to change, and carry on with goals in the face of difficulty is known as resilience. Creating coping mechanisms, staying optimistic, and concentrating on solutions rather than problems are all part of building resilience. Resilient people, for instance, focus on the actions they can do to handle the situation, look for support, and maintain hope for the future when faced with a personal setback like a health condition or a job loss. People with resilience can better control their stress, get beyond challenges, and stay motivated when things get hard. People with resilience can better deal with setbacks and draw insightful conclusions.

Moreover, identifying and questioning limiting assumptions and ideas is frequently necessary while learning from trying circumstances. Negative thought patterns, known as limiting beliefs, can impede personal development and keep people from completely accepting challenges. For instance, a person who feels unfit to be a team leader could shy away from assuming such responsibilities even when they present themselves. People can let go of their limiting beliefs and become more receptive to new experiences by recognizing and confronting them. This process includes raising doubts about the integrity of these ideas, looking into different viewpoints, and acting to overcome obstacles you put on yourself. People can increase their potential and tackle challenging circumstances more openly and confidently by resolving their limiting beliefs.

A crucial component of gaining knowledge from challenging circumstances is developing self-compassion. During difficult times, self-compassion entails being kind, patient, and understanding to oneself. It is crucial to understand that challenges and setbacks are normal aspects of being human and that passing judgment on oneself and oneself harshly is not constructive. For instance, practicing self-compassion entails accepting the effort made, realizing that failures are a typical part of progress, and refraining from blaming oneself if someone fails to meet a goal. People can preserve a positive self-image, better handle stress, and address upcoming obstacles with a constructive perspective by practicing self-compassion.

When learning from challenging events, it's crucial to use other people's help in addition to these tactics. Support systems, including friends, family, mentors, and experts in the field, can offer insight, support, and direction. Interacting with these support networks can provide insightful information, consoling, and useful guidance on overcoming obstacles. For instance, talking through a challenging circumstance with a reliable mentor can help clarify the best course of action and provide comfort when things seem unclear. By utilizing the assistance of others, people can improve their capacity to absorb knowledge and get over challenging circumstances.

Being proactive and introspective is necessary for the ongoing and growing process of learning from challenging circumstances. This process involves adopting a growth mindset, reflecting on experiences, getting feedback, putting insights to use, developing resilience, confronting limiting beliefs, practicing self-compassion, and utilizing support. By using these techniques, people can improve their professional and personal development, turn setbacks into learning opportunities, and overcome barriers in the future with more assurance and efficiency.

Ultimately, having the capacity to draw lessons from challenging circumstances is an important talent that promotes achievement and general well-being. By adopting an open-minded and receptive attitude toward problems, people can derive valuable insights, enhance their competencies, and cultivate constructive transformation. Adversity can be used as a springboard for personal development through ongoing introspection and development, laying the groundwork for future successes and a more contented existence.

CHAPTER V

Building Resilience and Positive Mindsets

The Power of Resilience

The extraordinary capacity to overcome hardship, adjust to change, and persevere in the face of difficulties is known as resilience. It is a fundamental characteristic that gives people the ability to persevere and handle life's unavoidable ups and downs with strength. Resilience is powerful because it can turn obstacles into learning experiences and give people a renewed feeling of hope and resolve that helps them go forward. The essence of resilience, its significance in both personal and professional life, and methods for developing and strengthening resilience to thrive in the face of adversity are all covered in this section.

The ability to handle stress and adversity on a psychological and emotional level is a common definition of resilience. It is a dynamic process encompassing attitudes, behaviors, and actions that may be acquired and enhanced over time rather than an innate quality. Resilience is fundamentally about keeping a good mindset and taking initiative when faced with obstacles. Resilient people, for example, concentrate on finding answers and retaining hope rather than giving up when faced with a big life event, like losing their career or suffering a personal loss. Even in the most trying situations, they can recognize chances for growth and development because of their optimistic outlook.

Adaptability is one of the main components of resilience. Because life is unpredictable, adjusting to new situations is essential for surviving uncertainty. Being adaptable is having an open mind, being prepared to change viewpoints, and having the flexibility to adapt plans as circumstances demand. For instance, many people and organizations had to adjust to new living, working quickly, and learning methods during the COVID-19 pandemic. Resilience was shown by those who could adapt to these changes and develop innovative solutions for brand-new problems. Being adaptable enables people to be resourceful and flexible, transforming challenges into chances for advancement and development.

Emotional control is a crucial aspect of resilience. Emotional regulation and expression skills are critical for preserving mental health and well-being. Resilient people can acknowledge and process emotions like fear, rage, and sadness without overwhelming them. Resilient people, for example, permit themselves to feel the related emotions following a setback, such as a failed project or a personal disappointment. Still, they do not allow these sentiments to control their behavior. Rather, they process their feelings and recover equilibrium using coping mechanisms like writing, mindfulness, or chatting with a close friend. People with emotional regulation are better able to handle obstacles because it keeps them calm and in control.

Resilience also depends critically on social support. A strong support system and relationships can offer consolation, practical help, and a feeling of community when things are hard. When faced with hardship, for instance, having friends, family, or coworkers to lean on can make all the difference in the world. These connections serve as stress relievers and are a great source of coping mechanisms. Furthermore, belonging to an encouraging group encourages a sense of camaraderie and assistance to one another, which can improve resilience all around. People's capacity to handle stress and bounce back from losses can be strengthened by actively seeking out and sustaining strong relationships.

Having meaning and purpose in life is another aspect of resilience. Even in the face of difficulty, having a distinct sense of purpose may give direction and drive. People can find meaning in their experiences and a motivation to keep going when they have a purpose. People with a strong sense of purpose that propels them ahead, such as those who are enthusiastic about their careers, devoted to a cause, or devoted to their families, are frequently more resilient. This sense of purpose can serve as an anchor in tumultuous times, giving stability and the will to overcome obstacles. People can develop a stronger sense of purpose and improve their resilience by ensuring their behaviors are consistent with their values and objectives.

Developing the ability to flourish despite stress and adversity is what resilience is all about, not avoiding them. Developing a growth mindset—where setbacks are seen as chances for growth and learning—is essential to developing resilience. For instance, resilient people perceive failure as an opportunity to grow rather than a reflection of their shortcomings. Curiosity and a willingness to take chances are encouraged by this growth-oriented viewpoint and are necessary for both professional and personal development. By accepting obstacles as chances for personal growth, people can strengthen their resilience and acquire the ability to deal with future hardships.

Resilience can be built by practicing self-care, problem-solving techniques, and reasonable goal-setting. Efficient problem-solving includes determining the underlying reasons for an obstacle, formulating possible fixes, and resolving the problem. For example, breaking down a difficulty into manageable parts and getting advice from coworkers can help someone with trouble solving a work-related issue. Resilience also depends on self-care, including leading a healthy lifestyle, exercising frequently, and partaking in enjoyable and calming activities. Self-care simplifies handling difficulties by lowering stress and recharging one's physical and emotional vitality. Establishing attainable goals gives people a feeling of purpose and achievement, which keeps them motivated and focused through trying times. People can increase their resilience by gaining momentum and confidence by setting small but attainable goals and acknowledging their accomplishments.

Cultivating thankfulness and optimism also contributes to resilience. Even in difficult circumstances, optimism entails holding an optimistic view and anticipating success. Resilient people, for instance, discover methods to generate positive experiences even in the face of hardship by concentrating on what they can control. By encouraging a positive outlook, practicing thankfulness—such as writing in a gratitude diary or thanking others—can also strengthen resilience. Being grateful enables people to concentrate on the positive aspects of their lives, which can offer consolation and perspective when things are tough. People can develop a more resilient mindset and positively tackle situations by practicing thankfulness and optimism.

To sum up, resilience is a strong attribute that helps people overcome obstacles, adjust to change, and overcome difficulties. It combines adaptability, emotional control, purpose, social support, optimistic thinking, and doable tactics. Through developing these resilience-boosting skills, people can improve their capacity to handle stress, bounce back from failures, and prosper in the face of hardship. Instead of avoiding difficulties, resilience is the ability to see them as chances for personal progress. A support network, self-care, and ongoing learning can help people develop and sustain resilience, promoting success in their personal and professional lives. Resilience can turn adversity into opportunity by encouraging a spirit of strength, hope, and resolve that enables people to move on in the face of adversity.

Mindfulness and Positivity

Positive thinking and mindfulness are two related ideas that greatly impact life satisfaction and general well-being. Being present and involved in the moment is the practice of mindfulness, which enables people to experience life more fully and successfully manage stress. Cultivating positivity, or an optimistic attitude, improves mental and emotional well-being. Positive thinking and mindfulness promote increased resilience, fulfillment, and happiness. This section examines the ideas of positivity and mindfulness, their advantages, and workable methods for applying them to everyday life.

Originating in traditional meditation techniques, mindfulness has become widely acknowledged in contemporary psychology and wellness domains. It entails being mindful of the here and now while maintaining an open, curious, and nonjudgmental mindset. By keeping an eye on the present moment, mindfulness assists people in escaping the never-ending loop of past and future thoughts that frequently cause tension and worry. To completely engage with their present experience, a person practicing mindfulness could, for instance, concentrate on their breathing, their body's sensations, or the sounds in their environment. This concentrated concentration lessens the effects of stressors and improves general mental health by fostering a sense of clarity and serenity.

Reducing stress is one of the main advantages of mindfulness. Persistent stress is a widespread condition that has been linked to heart disease, depression, anxiety, and other health issues. By encouraging calm and a sense of control over one's thoughts and emotions, mindfulness helps to reduce stress. By engaging in mindfulness practices, people can learn to notice their thoughts and feelings without being consumed. This separation makes a more balanced reaction to stimuli possible, which also stops negative feelings from worsening. For example, practicing mindfulness can assist someone who is experiencing anxiety in acknowledging their feelings without allowing them to control their thoughts or behavior. Mindfulness improves health and well-being by promoting a peaceful awareness that lessens stress's psychological and physiological effects.

Conversely, positivism is the discipline of keeping an optimistic mindset and emphasizing life's positive elements. It entails nurturing happy feelings like pleasure, thankfulness, and hope, which greatly impact life satisfaction and general happiness. It is not necessary to ignore life's obstacles to think positively; instead, one should approach them with a constructive mindset. For instance, a positive thinker could concentrate on lessons learned and future improvements rather than obsess over mistakes. This upbeat viewpoint promotes resilience, allowing people to overcome obstacles skillfully and recover from losses more rapidly.

Positive thinking has advantages for relationships, physical and mental health, and all aspects of life. Positive emotions have been linked to improved immunological response, less inflammatory response, and a decreased risk of developing chronic illnesses. Positive thinking also makes people more inclined to practice good habits like consistent exercise, a balanced diet, and enough sleep, all of which improve general health. When it comes to mental health, optimism works to offset the damaging effects of negative thought patterns that can result in anxiety and sadness. People can cultivate a sense of drive and hope by emphasizing the positive aspects of life, which is crucial for their mental and emotional health.

Since mindfulness can foster a happy outlook, positivity and mindfulness are closely related concepts. People presented and involved in the moment can recognize and value the little pleasures and good things that might otherwise go undetected. As part of a mindfulness exercise, someone might, for example, pause to appreciate the flavor of their favorite dish, the warmth of the sun on their skin, or the sound of birds singing. These instances of appreciation have the power to cultivate thankfulness and contentment, which can lead to a more optimistic view of life. Furthermore, mindfulness enables people to recognize and confront harmful thought patterns by increasing their awareness of their thoughts and feelings. People might focus on constructive and good thoughts by only monitoring their thoughts without passing judgment, which helps to foster an optimistic mindset.

Daily practice and dedication are necessary to integrate positivism and mindfulness. Meditating is one efficient approach to practicing mindfulness. Sitting still and concentrating on your breathing, your body's sensations, or a particular object of attention is the practice of mindfulness meditation. As the mind naturally strayed, the practitioner gently brought their attention back to the here and now. Frequent meditation can improve mindfulness, resulting in more peace and clarity all day. Furthermore, ordinary tasks like eating, walking, and even doing the dishes can be done with mindfulness. People can integrate mindfulness into their daily routines by giving these tasks full attention and using their senses.

Positive affirmations, acts of kindness, and gratitude journals are a few techniques that can foster positivity. Writing down the things for which one is thankful in a gratitude diary might help one turn their attention from the bad things in life to the good ones. Writing about a benevolent friend, a stunning sunset, or a personal achievement may encourage gratitude and optimism. Positive affirmations are declarations that uphold self-esteem and confidence in one's skills. Affirmations like "I am capable," "I am worthy," or "I can handle challenges," for example, can be repeated to assist in developing confidence and a good self-image. By creating a sense of community and goodwill, deeds of kindness like lending a hand to a neighbor, volunteering, or expressing gratitude to others can also boost optimism.

Positive thinking and mindfulness are effective strategies for raising general well-being and quality of life. People can create a sense of peace and presence, lessen stress, and enhance mental clarity by engaging in mindfulness practices. Conversely, positivity promotes resilience, improves psychological and physical well-being, and cultivates a feeling of contentment and satisfaction. Combined, these techniques have a synergistic impact that encourages a healthy, well-rounded response to life's obstacles. People can cultivate the abilities and mindset required to manage life with greater ease, joy, and resilience by introducing mindfulness and positivity into everyday routines.

In conclusion, having a positive outlook and practicing mindfulness is critical to living a long and healthy life. Positive thinking and the cultivation of happy feelings are the major goals of positivism, whereas mindfulness is being present and involved at the moment. Numerous advantages come with both techniques, such as lowered stress levels, better physical and mental health, and increased general well-being. People can change how they interact with the world and themselves by regularly practicing positivity and mindfulness, which will increase their fulfillment, resilience, and happiness. Living a more positive and mindful life is a significant step toward living a more balanced and fulfilling existence where chances for growth are fully realized, and challenges are faced with grace.

Overcoming Negative Thought Patterns

Negative thought patterns can have a serious negative effect on one's general and mental well-being. If left unchecked, these patterns—which are frequently typified by habitual, illogical, and negative thoughts—can result in persistent stress, anxiety, and melancholy. Identifying and combating negative thinking patterns, cultivating a more optimistic outlook, and forming better cognitive habits are all necessary to overcome negative thought patterns. To enhance mental health and quality of life, this section investigates the nature of negative thought patterns, their impacts, and methods for overcoming them.

Cognitive distortions, another name for negative thought patterns, are automatic, frequently prejudiced, and erroneous ways of thinking. Some distortions are all-or-nothing thinking, overgeneralization, mental filtering, discounting the positive, leaping to judgments, exaggeration, and reduction, emotive reasoning, should statements, labeling and mislabeling, and personalization. For instance, all-or-nothing thinking sees everything in stark contrast to one another, ignoring any in-between. Thinking, "I failed this test, so I am a complete failure," as opposed to realizing that a single test does not accurately represent one's entire aptitude, is an example of this. Such skewed thinking might exacerbate mental health problems by spreading a generalized feeling of pessimism and hopelessness.

Negative thought patterns have a wide range of consequences. Because those who engage in these habits are more prone to see events as threatening or impossible, they can result in heightened tension and worry. For instance, someone who often draws inferences could automatically anticipate the worst in social situations, which could increase their social anxiety and feelings of loneliness. As the person gets caught in a vicious cycle of self-criticism and hopelessness, these negative ideas might eventually lead to the onset of depression. Furthermore, negative thought patterns can erode one's sense of self-worth and self-efficacy, making it challenging to set and achieve objectives and lead fulfilling lives. This might exacerbate the negative thought pattern by creating a feeling of helplessness and immobility.

The first step to breaking unfavorable thought patterns is realizing them. This entails cultivating mindfulness and self-awareness to recognize these thoughts when they arise. Mindfulness exercises like meditation can help people become more aware of their thoughts and identify cognitive distortions. In a mindfulness meditation session, for instance, one can notice the emergence of self-doubt or criticism and recognize them as negative thinking patterns instead of objective truths. People can detach themselves from these thoughts and lessen their influence on their feelings and actions by observing them without judgment.

The next stage is confronting and reframing unfavorable thought patterns after they have been identified. This entails weighing the arguments in favor of and against these ideas and considering alternate, more impartial viewpoints. Cognitive-behavioral therapy (CBT) methods work very well. CBT helps people challenge the integrity of their negative ideas and swap them out for more logical and helpful ones. If someone thinks, "I'll never succeed at this job," they can refute this notion by citing prior accomplishments and abilities. They might also consider other reasons for their current problems, including a momentary setback instead of an ongoing failure. People can lessen their emotional suffering and cultivate a more optimistic perspective by rephrasing negative beliefs.

It takes constant use of these approaches until they become second nature to develop improved cognitive habits. Since it takes time and effort to change deeply ingrained cognitive habits, this needs patience and commitment. Maintaining a thought diary is a useful tactic where people may document their negative ideas, the circumstances around them, and the steps they took to challenge and reframe them. With continued use, this technique can lessen negative ideas' frequency and power while supporting more balanced thought patterns. People can also practice positive self-talk, which involves purposefully substituting positive phrases and affirmations for negative ideas. For example, they can tell themselves, "I am capable and learning every day," rather than, "I'm not good enough."

Addressing the underlying ideas underlying negative thinking patterns is crucial to breaking free from harmful thought patterns. Negative thinking habits frequently stem from firmly held views about oneself, others, and the world. These ideas may result from learned behaviors, cultural influences, or prior experiences. For instance, someone who was raised in a harsh atmosphere could have come to believe that they are imperfect and undeserving from the beginning. People must do in-depth introspection and, in certain situations, seek treatment to examine and rethink these fundamental ideas if they are to alter these underlying ones. People can permanently change their cognitive patterns and general mindset by addressing the underlying causes of unfavorable thought patterns.

Developing thankfulness and concentrating on good memories further create a positive outlook. Gratitude exercises, like journaling about your blessings or thanking others daily, can assist in turning your attention from the bad things in life to the good stuff in it. Writing down three things for which one is thankful every day, for instance, can assist people in improving their attitude and lessening the influence of their negative thoughts. Participating in joyful and fulfilling activities, including volunteering, socializing, or taking up a hobby, can also improve general well-being and strengthen positive thought patterns.

A further essential component in breaking bad thought patterns is self-compassion. Self-compassion is being compassionate and understanding, especially when facing challenges or failures. Instead of severe self-criticism, self-compassion helps people see their shared humanity and treat themselves with empathy. For example, if someone makes a mistake, they can remind themselves, "It's okay to make mistakes; everyone does," rather than, "I'm so stupid." I'm able to grow from this and go on. People can lessen the intensity of their negative thoughts and create a more nourishing and encouraging internal dialogue by engaging in self-compassion practices.

In summary, changing unfavorable thought habits is crucial to enhancing mental health and well-being. The key to escaping the negative cycle is to identify and confront these beliefs and cultivate a positive outlook and better cognitive habits. In this process, gratitude, positive self-talk, self-compassion, mindfulness exercises, and cognitive behavioral therapy are crucial. By adopting these techniques and resolving underlying beliefs that give rise to negative thought patterns, people can change the way they think, lessen emotional suffering, and improve their quality of life. Although changing one's negative thought patterns takes time and perseverance, developing a more resilient and cheerful outlook makes the work worthwhile.

Stress Management Strategies

Stress is an inevitable part of contemporary life. While stress in moderation can boost performance and motivate people, prolonged stress can harm one's physical and emotional well-being. Using efficient stress-reduction techniques is crucial to preserving general well-being and raising the standard of living. This section examines several stress-reduction strategies, such as mindfulness, physical activity, time management, social support, relaxation methods, and lifestyle modifications.

One effective strategy for stress management is mindfulness. It entails giving the present moment your attention and being involved without judgment. One can practice mindfulness through meditation by paying attention to one breath or a particular object and gently bringing their mind back to it whenever it wanders. By encouraging relaxation and a sense of control over one's thoughts and emotions, this practice aids in reducing stress. A mindfulness meditation session, for example, can induce a state of calmness that lessens the physiological impacts of stress, such as elevated blood pressure and heart rate. Incorporating mindfulness into routine tasks like walking, eating, and even doing the dishes is also possible. People can build mindfulness in their daily routines and lower their overall stress levels by giving these tasks full attention and using their senses.

Another good way to manage stress is to exercise. The body's natural mood enhancers, endorphins, are produced more when exercising, and the stress hormone cortisol is released at lower amounts. Frequent exercise helps mental health by lowering anxiety and depression in addition to improving physical health. Exercises that increase heart rate, like swimming, cycling, or running, counteract the negative effects of stress by enhancing self-esteem and providing a sense of accomplishment. Furthermore, exercising offers a constructive way to relieve stress and annoyance. Including physical activity in one's daily routine can greatly lower stress levels and enhance general well-being, even if it's just a little stroll during lunch.

To reduce stress, time management skills are essential. Ineffective time management can exacerbate stress by causing overwhelming emotions and an unwavering sense of urgency. One can make their chores more organized and less stressful by prioritizing them, making realistic goals, and breaking down larger activities into smaller, more manageable pieces. For example, setting deadlines and tasks in a planner or digital calendar can help people remain on track and lessen the stress of last-minute rushes. Furthermore, time management strategies like the Pomodoro Technique, which divides work into intervals with brief pauses in between, can enhance productivity and focus while lowering the general stress of heavy workloads.

Another important component in stress management is social support. Connecting with friends, family, or support groups can help people deal with stress more skillfully by offering practical and emotional support. For instance, discussing issues with a reliable friend might bring comfort and fresh insight into managing tense circumstances. In addition, engaging in social activities can provide a release from stress and a chance to unwind and relish good times. Social engagement and developing a solid support system can improve resilience and lessen the negative effects of stress in one's life.

Stress can also be effectively managed by using relaxation techniques such as progressive muscle relaxation, deep breathing, and visualization. Taking slow, deep breaths and deep breathing exercises helps to lower heart rate, induce relaxation, and foster a calmer, more relaxed state of being. To help relieve the physical tension brought on by stress, progressive muscle relaxation entails tensing and relaxing various bodily muscle groups. By using visualization techniques, people can promote relaxation by mentally escaping from stressful situations and entering a serene place. By using these strategies regularly, people can better control their acute stress and avoid developing chronic stress.

Modifications to one's lifestyle can also be quite helpful in stress management. The body may handle stress better if a balanced diet, enough sleep, and abstinence from alcohol and caffeine are followed. For example, stress can be lessened by eating a balanced diet of fruits, vegetables, whole grains, and lean proteins, which can supply the nutrients needed for optimum physical and mental health. Since sleep loss can worsen stress and impair cognitive performance, getting enough sleep is essential for managing stress. Stress levels can be decreased, and sleep quality enhanced by establishing a regular sleep schedule and providing a comfortable sleeping environment. Reducing the intake of depressants like alcohol and stimulants like caffeine can also stop these substances' detrimental effects on stress and general well-being.

Participating in joyful and fulfilling hobbies and activities is another crucial component of stress management. Following hobbies and interests can mitigate the negative impacts of stress by giving one a sense of purpose and satisfaction. Painting, gardening, playing an instrument, reading, and other hobbies, for instance, can offer a mental retreat from stress and foster chances for enjoyment and relaxation. Prioritizing self-care and scheduling leisure time can improve general well-being and lower stress levels.

Effective stress management techniques can also involve cognitive-behavioral techniques. These strategies allow negative thought patterns to be recognized, contested, and replaced with more realistic, upbeat ideas. For instance, when faced with an overwhelming job project, someone may change their perspective from "I can't handle this" to "I can break this down into smaller steps and manage it one step at a time." People can lessen stress's emotional toll on them and approach circumstances with more resilience and confidence by altering how they think. Furthermore, cultivating thankfulness through journaling and concentrating on life's blessings can help people refocus their attention from worries to the things that make them happy and fulfilled.

Lastly, a key component of stress management is getting expert assistance when required. Counselors, therapists, and support groups can offer invaluable direction and aid for stress management. With techniques and resources catered to each person's unique requirements, professional assistance can help people create healthy coping skills and enhance their general well-being. For example, mindfulness-based stress reduction (MBSR) teaches mindfulness and relaxation practices, while cognitive-behavioral therapy (CBT) assists people in recognizing and altering harmful thought patterns. Getting assistance is a proactive approach to stress management and can offer the sustained support required for long-term well-being.

In summary, stress management is essential to preserving general health and well-being. A few effective methods for lowering stress and enhancing quality of life include mindfulness, physical activity, time management, social support, relaxation techniques, and lifestyle modifications. People can develop healthy coping strategies and resilience by adopting them into their routines and obtaining expert assistance when necessary. Although overcoming stress is a journey that takes dedication and work, the rewards of less stress and more well-being make the effort worthwhile. People may easily deal with life's obstacles and have healthy, satisfying lives with regular practice and support.

Gratitude and Optimism

Gratitude and optimism are two strong psychological qualities that can greatly improve someone's quality of life. The beneficial effects of both qualities on relationships, general well-being, and physical and mental health have been well-studied. This section delves into the characteristics of thankfulness and optimism, their advantages, and doable methods for developing these qualities to promote a more robust and satisfying existence.

Appreciating the positive aspects of one's life, no matter how tiny or large, is the essence of gratitude. It entails appreciating and appreciating life's positive aspects despite its difficulties. Gratitude creates a sense of wealth and contentment by turning attention from what is lacking to what is present. This change in viewpoint can have a significant impact on mental health, lowering anxiety and depressive symptoms while raising happiness levels all around. For instance, people who consistently practice thankfulness report feeling happier, having a higher quality of sleep, and experiencing more good feelings. Having gratitude makes it easier to be in the now rather than dwelling on complaints from the past or concerns about the future.

Conversely, optimism is the widespread belief that positive things will occur. Those who are optimistic typically think of obstacles as transient and manageable, and they also believe that obstacles can have a positive impact. Optimists are more likely to take the initiative to solve problems and ask for help when they do, which can result in improved stress management. According to research, numerous positive health outcomes, such as a decreased risk of cardiovascular disease, a more robust immune system, and longer life spans, have been linked to optimism. In addition, optimists are more likely to practice good habits like quitting smoking, eating a balanced diet, and exercising frequently, all of which improve their general well-being.

Gratitude and optimism have a synergistic relationship. By cultivating a positive attitude and highlighting positive experiences, practicing thankfulness can increase one's sense of optimism. On the other hand, those with an optimistic outlook are more likely to notice and value the positive aspects of their environment, which might facilitate feelings of gratitude. Because of their mutually reinforcing and amplifying effects, appreciation and optimism generate a positive feedback loop that increases resilience and overall pleasure.

A useful method for developing thankfulness is to maintain a gratitude diary. This is keeping a gratitude journal, where one writes down everything from big life events to little everyday joys. Taking note of the pleasure of a sunny day, a friend's encouragement, or a filling dinner, for example, might foster the development of a habit of identifying and valuing good experiences. Studies have indicated that people who keep gratitude diaries report feeling better about themselves, their relationships, and their stress levels. By continuously focusing on them, people can educate their brains to notice and value more positive events. This will increase feelings of optimism and thankfulness.

Expressing gratitude to others is another powerful way to cultivate thankfulness. Thank-you notes, vocal acknowledgments, and deeds of compassion can all accomplish this. Not only can expressing appreciation improve relationships, but it also improves the well-being of the giver and the recipient. For instance, expressing gratitude to a coworker for their assistance with a project can enhance collaboration and workplace morale while also elevating the giver's mood and reaffirming their sense of social support. These acts of appreciation foster a supportive social atmosphere where generosity and appreciation proliferate, ultimately improving the group's well-being.

Moreover, mindfulness training can increase optimism and thankfulness. By focusing on the here and now without passing judgment, mindfulness enables people to experience and enjoy their environment completely. People who practice mindfulness can notice good things more often when they happen instead of ignoring or taking them for granted. For example, mindful eating promotes chewing slowly and appreciating each bite, which increases food enjoyment and appreciation. In a similar vein, mindfulness can assist people in recognizing and appreciating the wonders of the natural world, the warmth of a loved one's smile, or the accomplishment of a task well done. A stronger sense of thankfulness and optimism may result from this increased awareness of and appreciation for good things in life.

Several behavioral and cognitive techniques can be used to foster optimism. Positive visualization is a useful strategy that involves helping people see successful outcomes for their obstacles and ambitions. This method can increase self-assurance and motivation, increasing the likelihood that people will take the initiative to reach their goals. For instance, imagining a well-received presentation might ease nervousness and boost confidence since the presenter feels more prepared and capable. An optimistic mindset is reinforced by a positive vision, which makes it simpler to keep a positive attitude in the face of difficulties.

Rephrasing pessimistic ideas is another effective way to promote optimism. This entails recognizing and confronting negative or gloomy ideas and substituting them with realistic and upbeat ones. In this context, cognitive-behavioral methods like cognitive restructuring can be especially useful. For example, one can reframe the thought, "I'll never get this right," to, "I'm learning and improving, and with effort, I can succeed." Pessimism can be lessened, and a more positive view can be developed by continuously confronting and rephrasing negative thoughts.

Finally, it should be noted that optimism and thankfulness are strong character attributes that can greatly improve relationships, mental and physical health, and general well-being. People can develop a sense of abundance and satisfaction through journaling, expressing gratitude, and engaging in mindfulness practices. Similarly, people can cultivate optimism by engaging in worthwhile activities, reframing negative ideas, practicing positive imagery, and creating a network of supporting people. Gratitude and optimism have a reciprocal relationship that produces a positive feedback loop in which each quality amplifies and supports the other, increasing resilience and general happiness. Although cultivating these qualities takes time and constant effort, the rewards of a more robust and full life make the effort worthwhile.

CHAPTER VI

Creating Positive Environments

Establishing Healthy Boundaries

Setting appropriate boundaries is crucial to preserving one's well-being and developing wholesome relationships. Boundaries assist people in defending their mental, emotional, and physical space by defining the parameters of appropriate behavior. They guard against feelings of bitterness and burnout by making sure that interactions are civil and well-balanced. The significance of sound limits, their establishment, and their advantages are all covered in this section.

Sound boundaries are important for several reasons. First and foremost, they safeguard a person's sense of identity. Without boundaries, people could feel overburdened by other people's expectations and demands, which could cause tension and worry. Setting boundaries helps people put their wants and ideals first, preventing them from sacrificing their well-being for the benefit of other people. Limiting work hours, for example, can help keep a healthy work-life balance and avoid burnout. Boundaries enable people to uphold their integrity and express their rights by establishing what is and is not acceptable.

Communicating and being self-aware is necessary for setting limits. Determining one's boundaries and principles is the first step. This necessitates reflection and a sincere evaluation of what matters most to one's well-being. For instance, a person may realize that rude behavior is intolerable or require time to refuel. After establishing these boundaries, they must be assertively and explicitly stated to others. This might be difficult, particularly for those afraid of being rejected or confronted.

Nonetheless, setting and upholding boundaries depend on efficient communication. Expressing one's wants with "I" words can assist avoid coming across as judgmental. For example, it's more productive to state, "I need some time to myself after work," rather than "You are always bothering me."

Setting and upholding boundaries are equally crucial. It's vital always to respect boundaries that have been set. Saying no to requests beyond one's comfort zone may be part of this. It's critical to remember that establishing limits is a sign of mutual respect and self-respect rather than selfishness. For example, gently reminding someone that polite communication is required if they frequently interrupt during conversations can help to enforce the boundary. Setting and maintaining boundaries also entails intervening when they are consistently crossed. This could entail removing oneself from unhealthy connections or asking a mentor or counselor for assistance.

Setting up appropriate boundaries has many advantages. Better mental and emotional wellness is one of the biggest benefits. Boundaries foster a sense of security and control, which lowers tension and anxiety. When people learn to value and safeguard their needs, they also help them develop a stronger sense of self-worth and self-respect. Moreover, partnerships with sound limits are more satisfying. Clear communication of boundaries promotes respect and understanding among people. Deeper connections and more harmonious, encouraging relationships may result from this. For example, a friendship with mutual respect for boundaries is likely more satisfying and long-lasting than one where boundaries are consistently crossed.

Healthy limits not only promote personal well-being but also enhance career success. Establishing clear limits at work can improve output and job happiness. By making sure that job obligations do not interfere with personal time or well-being, they help to prevent burnout. Boundaries can be placed around work hours and tasks to avoid the negative impacts of overwork and preserve a healthy work-life balance. Boundaries also encourage justice and respect in the workplace. They lessen misunderstandings and confrontations by ensuring everyone knows their roles and duties.

Setting up good boundaries is crucial to safeguarding one's well-being and cultivating wholesome relationships. It entails self-awareness, lucid communication, and uniform application. Maintaining boundaries can improve mental and emotional well-being, self-esteem, and more satisfying relationships. In the workplace, setting limits can help to maintain respect and equity while preventing burnout. We may design a more balanced, courteous, and meaningful existence by acknowledging and respecting both our own and other people's boundaries.

Fostering Positive Relationships

Developing healthy relationships is not just a choice, but a key to unlocking a happier and more fulfilling life. These connections offer more than just company and support; they enhance our mental and physical health and boost our overall life satisfaction. By embracing fundamental values like trust, empathy, respect, and good communication, we can foster these kinds of relationships and reap the benefits they bring.

Positive relationships are built on effective communication. It is easier to avoid misunderstandings and settle disputes when there is clear, honest, and polite communication. It entails listening to other people as well as expressing oneself. Particularly crucial is active listening, which is carefully considering what is being said and listening intently. The other person will feel appreciated and understood if you listen to them intently and with attention. For instance, honestly listening to and answering a friend's worries builds a stronger bond and sense of trust. Regularly expressing gratitude and affection also contributes to effective communication and helps to fortify the relationship between people.

Empathy, the ability to understand and share the feelings of another, is a crucial component of positive relationships. It promotes compassion and support, allowing us to connect with others on a deeper emotional level. By putting ourselves in someone else's shoes, we can respond to their needs and feelings more sympathetically. For instance, acknowledging a coworker's concern and offering assistance can strengthen professional relationships. Positive relationships thrive on a sense of connection and reciprocal caring, which empathy fosters.

Respect for one another is essential to a happy partnership. Respect entails appreciating one another's viewpoints, emotions, and limits. It involves being considerate and courteous to others, even when disagreeing. Both people feel appreciated and understood in a respectful relationship, which promotes security and trust. Respecting one another's individuality and desire for personal space, for example, can reduce conflict and increase intimacy in love relationships. A more contented and peaceful relationship also results from respecting one another's peculiarities and unique viewpoints.

Positive relationships are constructed on a foundation of trust. Being trustworthy requires consistency, honesty, and dependability. It is acquired over time by deeds that exhibit reliability and integrity. People in relationships feel safe and certain when they have mutual trust. Open communication, vulnerability, and stronger emotional ties are made possible by this security. Strong bonds of loyalty and trust are formed, for instance, when someone regularly fulfills their commitments and supports a friend in difficult circumstances. To build trust and avoid misunderstandings, it is equally important to be open and truthful.

In summary, cultivating healthy relationships demands commitment to clear communication, empathy, respect for one another, and trust. These components build a solid basis for companionship, emotional support, and community relationships. Good connections add meaning to our lives and improve our general happiness and well-being. People can build rewarding and durable connections in the face of adversity by putting these ideas into practice.

Positivity at Work and a Life of Positivity

Being positive at work is essential to a successful career and makes a big difference in leading a positive life. A positive atmosphere in the workplace fosters a sense of worth, motivation, and engagement among staff members. This good environment fosters a holistic understanding of well-being and contentment among employees, improving productivity and teamwork and permeating into their personal lives.

Establishing a culture of respect and gratitude is the first step toward creating a healthy work environment.

Employee morale is raised, and a sense of community is strengthened when efforts and accomplishments are acknowledged through official recognition programs or sincere expressions of gratitude. Employee motivation and dedication are more likely to increase when they feel valued. This appreciation-based culture creates a positive feedback loop that motivates team members to continue working together excellently. For instance, a manager who consistently recognizes the accomplishments and contributions of their team builds a motivated and encouraging work environment.

Another essential component of cheerfulness at work is effective communication. Clear, truthful, and courteous communication minimizes misinterpretations and fosters confidence. Employees are encouraged to voice their problems and suggestions when there is no fear of retaliation when there is open communication. In addition to empowering people, this transparency promotes inclusion and respect for one another. Employees are more likely to collaborate successfully and settle disputes amicably in a setting where constructive communication is encouraged, promoting workplace harmony.

Encouraging employees' well-being is crucial to preserving optimism in the workplace. Businesses prioritizing employee mental and physical health by offering wellness programs, flexible scheduling, and work-life balance initiatives provide the groundwork for long-term success and contentment. Employee engagement and commitment to their work are more likely to persist when they see that their well-being is valued. Companies that support regular breaks provide access to mental health resources and encourage employees to take time off, for example, to show that they are committed to their workers' overall well-being. This support results from higher levels of contentment and lower stress levels.

Workplace positivity concepts can be easily transferred into personal life, resulting in an endless loop of good things happening to you. In personal connections, efficient communication, gratitude, and support for well-being are essential, just like in the job. Relationships with family and friends are strengthened, and problems are resolved more skillfully through open and honest communication. Expressing gratitude to those you love and care about builds relationships and creates a nurturing atmosphere. They prioritize self-care and well-being, guaranteeing that people have the stamina and fortitude to sustain constructive relationships in all spheres of life.

Adopting these values regularly is necessary to live a positive existence. It entails positively approaching obstacles and looking for answers rather than wallowing in them. It involves developing an attitude of thankfulness, appreciating life's blessings, and frequently expressing gratitude. People can design a life full of fulfilling experiences and meaningful relationships by incorporating the principles of effective communication, gratitude, and well-being support into their everyday routines.

In conclusion, there is a strong correlation between a positive life and a positive work environment. In addition to improving professional satisfaction, a positive work environment that fosters effective communication, gratitude, and support for well-being also improves personal contentment. People can cultivate a comprehensive sense of well-being and build a life full of rewarding experiences and connections by continuously adhering to these principles. This holistic approach to positivity guarantees a robust, contented, and well-balanced life at work and beyond.

CONCLUSION

By the time we reach the end of "Navigating Negativity: Strategies for Positive Encounters: Transforming Toxic Interactions into Opportunities for Growth," it is evident that dealing with negativity is both a science and an art. You now have a full arsenal from this book to turn negative interactions into learning experiences for yourself and your relationships.

The first step to effectively controlling negativity is realizing its origins and effects on our lives. You have learned to identify and deal with your triggers by developing self-awareness and emotional intelligence, which opens the door to more positive encounters. Conflict resolution and developing constructive dialogues depend on effective communication strategies, such as forceful and active listening.

It is necessary to recognize and deal with harmful behaviors while reinterpreting obstacles as chances for personal development to transform toxicity. You may resist negativity and keep an optimistic view by developing resilience and cultivating a positive mindset. This positive mindset is a beacon of hope; ensuring that your surroundings are positive and conducive to healthy limits can help you maintain these adjustments in the long run.

"Navigating Negativity" is a call to action as much as a guide. It motivates you to consistently implement these techniques in your day-to-day activities, transforming every setback into an opportunity for personal development. By adhering to these values, you may make your life and the lives of people around you more rewarding, respectful, and positive.

Thank you for buying and reading/listening to our book. If you found this book useful/helpful please take a few minutes and leave a review on the platform where you purchased our book. Your feedback matters greatly to us.